LIFE *of* LOVE

A Joyful Guide to Self and Sensuality

JULIE HILSEN

Cover and Illustrations by Jessica Murrell
Graphics created by Julie Hilsen using Canva Pro Creative Use License

An Imprint for GracePoint Publishing (www.GracePointPublishing.com)

GracePoint Matrix, LLC
624 S. Cascade Ave, Suite 201
Colorado Springs, CO 80903
www.GracePointMatrix.com
Email: Admin@GracePointMatrix.com
SAN # 991-6032

A Library of Congress Control Number has been requested for this work and is pending.

ISBN: 978-1-955272-04-9
eISBN: 978-1-955272-03-2

Books may be purchased for educational, business, or sales promotional use.
For bulk order requests and price schedule contact:
Orders@GracePointPublishing.com

TABLE OF CONTENTS

Note From the Author

I speak in the context of male and female relationships for ease of delivery. However, I realize there are many types of relationships involving people who deeply care about each other. Any concept I discuss can be applied to any consenting love relationship. I am in favor of any combination in which people bring out the best in each other and share in the spirit of love. I provide devotions for you; use them to center your intentions. You can ask for help from any higher source you believe in to help you on your way or just feel my concern and support for you through my words. I wrote these words for you with complete love in my heart and the best intentions for you. Divinity can be any higher power you believe in. If you don't believe in a higher power, it can be your highest self, your all-knowingness. This book was written to bring out the highest good. This intention can guide your adventure and give you trust in the highest outcome possible. Please use these messages to ask for the highest good for yourself and those around you.

The information in this book is provided as informational resources only and is not to be relied on or used for diagnostic or treatment of any condition. It does not substitute for medical or psychiatric care. Any new physical activity should be approved by a physician.

Introduction

Consider that there is more to life than what you have experienced. You were drawn to this book because you desire more. I love that! If you let me, I will take you on a quest to discover what you can be and how you can show up in your life. Please know that just because you have loved one way your entire life, does not mean it has to be that way for the rest of your life. Old connections can be released, and new magical perspectives can liberate you. The old connections may be dissolved from a current relationship so you can replenish what you have, or you may dissolve a current relationship because your soul contract has been met and it's time for both of you to share with someone else. Maybe it is time for you to be alone.

It's okay to be uncertain, and deep down you may know the way for you. I am not promising all the answers, but I hope you can use this book as a guide on your soul path. Take quiet time to reflect on my suggestions. If they feel right, use them to make your way. What you need will come to you as you seek it. The important thing is for you to come with the intention and hope for creating more joy and love in your life.

Humans have more resources than ever—we have technology, fuel efficient cars, communication highways that connect our ideas and currency, and all kinds of entertainment at our fingertips. And yet there is a crisis of polarity, negativity, and destructiveness going on in the world. Shootings keep making headlines. All over the world, attacks of terror and control dominate the news. Human trafficking is a real problem and thankfully the awareness of it has grown with more and more arrests. Our children are losing their innocence through exposure of sexual content, explicit songs, videos available online, and even direct sexual predators online. The divine feminine has been disregarded and disrespected. We are manipulated by supercomputers and algorithms, as many are addicted to the validation of how many likes or shares an image receives on social media. Marketing and political tactics control what we see and don't see on many social platforms.

The attention is addicting, and we carry around our addiction in our pockets with a constant connection to the source of our obsession. There is no peace in this constant, false affirmation. It is not reality, but a psychological and marketing scheme which seems to have gone wrong. Looking for love outside of ourselves and craving validation dilutes self-worth and manipulates our minds. We are searching for something better, and the old ways are falling down. Our hearts need to be free.

I care about you. You picked up this book and read this far for a reason. Thank you! There are no coincidences. This book has not found you by accident, but by attraction. I need to share these messages with you, and you need to share your love with the world. The Earth needs more love. People are lonely and craving acceptance, compassion, and connection. We need it. We have to show up for each other to change the isolation, but first, we have to show up for ourselves. You show up by honoring yourself and your needs. Self-care is not optional. Before all else, you need to understand your needs by being calm so you can sense what your body is telling you. You have a powerful mind, but it's essential to quiet your mind so your heart and body can give you information. Your mind will question and challenge you, but your heart and body will connect you to your reality. I have complete gratitude for your contribution. You are creating your life in real time. Thank you.

How to Use This Book

I created this book to be interactive and a guide for self-discovery. People are becoming more open and curious about receiving messages and help from the angels and higher sources but are not sure how to ask. I provide the words in devotions. Devotions are requests or prayer-like meditations to center your heart on the thing that you desire. Devotions also are a way to create a space for what you desire. Think of them as pretty vessels you are holding which will be filled up with your desires. Feel free to address the deity you most strongly identify with. Read them aloud or softly in a calm voice. You may also read them silently, mentally holding the words. You can complete a devotion at any time of the day. You may find a special time when you can be most centered and calm, or you may find the words soothing when you feel out of sorts. It's really up to you.

I channeled these devotions from the angels and The Council of Light for you. At other times the angels gave me messages for you. Everything is labeled so you don't have to guess. There are also action steps and activities to help you connect to yourself and to the loving beings who are constantly around you. The only prerequisite for communicating with your angels is to come with an open heart and from a place of love. You can read this book from start to finish or in any order and refer to sections as needed. You can even refer to actions, exercises, angel messages, and devotions using the indexes in the back. I suggest flipping through the whole book, so you know the general topics. Then, decide where you want to begin.

First Steps

I applaud you for taking this step. The bravery to look for more, question your current reality, and attract more joy can be a scary proposition. You are taking responsibility for your happiness and loving presence in the world. You will make a difference first for yourself and then for everyone around you.

Starting out is simple and everything you need is sitting right there with you. Simple may not be easy at first. It starts with being connected to your body, accepting, and cherishing your unique divinity. True joy, love, and sensuality comes from within and trusting in your completeness. I'm going to guide you to your true answers at this moment.

Connected by Our Individual Uniqueness

Deep in our core we are connected. We know it, but many have forgotten. Sometimes we try to buy connections by having material things. However, the only answer and true sustaining connection we can have is love. People ask me why I am so happy. I have had people get upset with me for being so happy. I must be on medication, naive, delusional, or clueless. I have been called a Pollyanna; I had to look up what the heck that meant! I have always felt a special connection to this earth, people, animals, and to myself. My soul led me here to share my gift, my light with those who seek it. Every time I try to hold it in or pretend that I fit in, I am miserable; I don't want to fit in. I want to be myself, just as I give you permission to be one hundred percent you. It hurts too much to keep it a secret any longer. I have a feeling you don't want to keep your special gifts a secret any longer either.

Rising Consciousness

As we are reaching new areas of awareness on this planet, it will help to understand the power of love. It's the direction of a new earth and higher achievements of abundance. It feels good and it's amazing to own your frequency and share it without reservation and fear. It's empowering and fun! I want to help you find your way and share it with the world. You can connect to a higher vibration from Source and use it to guide your life. It starts with you and then radiates to the people closest to you. Before you know it there is a community of people loving and caring for each other and feeling the vibration of true love and joyful connection. I can get lost in the concept. You will still feel lows and have challenges, but you won't stay in them. You will pull yourself out of a slump with the memory of your true expression, your values, and the intention to be in the state of love with total respect for all your emotions. I hope you will give yourself permission to join me on a quest for love.

Life of love is not a delusion. Love is real and really powerful in its wisdom. My gift is to feel—really feel—emotions. That gift has made me very sensual. I feel the highs and the lows acutely and I must deal with channeling the energy to flow in and out, because holding it in makes me ill. I have made myself faint, vomit, or spike a fever by attempting to control or limit my emotions. I have always been different, but I know everyone has things that make them different. I know I am here to love and teach about showing love. You can find your purpose by diving into your passions and sharing them. It's part of your soul contract, that unique contribution that only you can give because no one else can. People spend their lives trying to figure it out, but it's usually something that you do easily because it's just natural for you. It starts with honoring yourself by making space for self-care. Your soul is all knowing, wise, and good. It is your divine right to love and be abundant.

Life Lessons are in Your Challenges

Every challenge and obstacle in life is there for a reason: to teach us and guide us on a path to master them. And for what? To elevate us and share our mastery with others. Believe it or not, every challenge and irritating person or situation is part of your important journey.

For example, I learned to plaster a smile on my face as a veil because if I let the lower base vibrations in, they would also be plastered all over my face. There's a thing called conditioning. Society likes happy little girls; sad little girls get ignored. So, I learned to keep on the happy side, focusing on the positive emotions that were acceptable and hiding the dark ones by pushing them away. We have all done it. Our parents wanted us to survive so they taught us how to fit in and play small or only play big when it was socially acceptable. Maybe your parents told you not to be a crybaby and to suck it up. Perhaps you were offered a cookie or distraction when you were upset.

I believe many parents have trouble watching their children suffer. So instead of empowering a child to work through a difficulty, they offer candy or food to distract their child from the pain. I believe this is how many people develop emotional eating. If you find yourself looking for food to calm down, feel better, or escape, it's a real thing. Dealing with your patterns can help heal not only your body but also old wounds you never conquered or explored as a child. Even though they are years or decades old, they can hang on around you until you acknowledge them and move on.

Emotions are Clues

You learned to ignore being hurt and pushed on to please your parents and survive by their rules or simply distract yourself from the feelings. We all want to please our parents, however, ignoring your body's messages while focusing on pleasing others can really add up to significant health issues. Parents can easily do it subconsciously. They want to protect their children. Usually, it's quite subtle. Comments like, "Oh, Jessica is really pretty." To a child that may sound like, "You are not as pretty as Jessica." When in fact there are many types of beauty and there is a person who can't imagine living without you. Everyone has a different opinion of "pretty." It's up to us to find all our buried feelings again to be free and really happy. Loving and accepting all the parts of us, even the ones our parents wanted to protect us from, is how we tap into our unique and powerful gifts.

Action Step: Get Curious About Your Unique Reactions or Emotions

What are some things that make you different? Are these things defining you in a positive way or do you try to hide them?

If you were encouraged to explore the full range of your emotions, you would learn to relate to powerful emotions and move through them. Each person has a unique way of feeling and processing emotions and this process needs to be honored instead of suppressed. Holding things in or suppressing feelings, contributes to illness later in life. Sharing these different, unique parts of yourself opens you up to living a divine, unique, joyful, and abundant life. If you recognize and honor all the parts of yourself, while respecting others, you open up to a new life; a life in which you feel empowered and fulfilled. Accepting all the parts of yourself makes you free.

Pay Attention to Fear

While you honor all your emotions, pay close attention to times you are fearful. You will not be able to accept yourself if you are fearful. The states of fear and acceptance cannot coexist. If you can calm the fear and move on to accepting the reality of the situation you can be neutral and start fact gathering. What is true about this situation? Finding neutrality makes you free to problem solve and reason.

PART ONE

Your Loving Soul

Chapter 1

Calling in The Light

There is light all around you and light within you. You are a perfect design. Anything or person who suggests you are broken or flawed, is in complete error. How do I know this? Because you are here on Earth, and you have a purpose for being here. Especially if you feel like you are lost or misplaced, your light is needed.

Sharing and feeling your light is easy when things are going as expected. You are light as a feather. You are walking on sunshine, and nothing can stop you when things are just falling in place and going well. It's complete harmony. When you feel this harmony, you are living in your soul purpose. People will be more attracted to you, things will seem effortless, and you will feel great.

Finding Harmony and Love

A more challenging situation presents itself when you feel separate from the light and your soul. Your voice is small and muffled and you find it harder to breathe. You feel alone and things are sticky and heavy. Emotions show up in your body in many ways. For example, when you ignore your connection to your purpose and joy, you may end up feeling burnt out and exhausted. Staying in dis-harmony too long can result in dis-ease. We have all been there! However, these feelings of separation and despair are clues for you. Your difficulties are there to show you what needs attention in this world. They are your soul's action steps! Finding your inner strength and using your resources to create a solution makes you a master of joy. You are a pillar of light and love. Claiming your power and recognizing your divinity promotes love in the world. You can radiate and share the love you feel when it comes from deep in your heart. You are free to find it. All you need do is ask and act!

I want to guide you to discover your love frequency and harmony. Then help you spend more time in this state of connection. I want you to understand grace and the flow that comes from complete confidence in the divine feminine. Know that your soul is living in your human body. There will be times your harmony is derailed by events, people, or even your body's condition. The ultimate goal is to know your joy and harmony so well that you can reconnect to it quickly if you find yourself out of balance. I am so excited for you and the opportunities you will awaken in yourself. I want you to know that through this communication you will feel my love for you. I have infused this text with my care for you with loving messages given to me from our guides and angels. You may choose to send your love to me, and I will receive it. Together we will strengthen the love connection in our world and raise the love vibration.

Intention is Powerful

You can want things to happen in your life, wish for them, dream of them, but the action starts with your intention and giving yourself permission to have the life of your dreams. Visualize or feel what you want to happen: the perfect feelings of connection, grace, and wholeness. Then set an intention. Intention makes space for what you want. Action without intention can lead you to your desires, eventually. Action with intention is a superhighway to manifestation. You have an absolute abundance of love and support around you. Buckle up!

Action Step: Setting A LOVE Intention

Visualize deep pure love in your heart. Look to the places around you. Use your eyes to spread calm, accepting love to everything around you. In cherishing your surroundings, you take a big step in finding gratitude and joy in your everyday world. Just observe. Create a quiet calmness in everything you see. Choose to only see the light in each thing. Compliment the sky on its brilliance. Bow to the moon's gentle glow and the stars' subtle sparkle. Smile at the green grass and the breeze. Smell your food and let the tastes swirl on your tongue in delight of the earth's bounty. The textures and flavors are endless for you to experience and cherish. Touch the fabrics around you. Enjoy the feel and smell of fresh washed clothing on your skin. Feel how your acknowledgments warm your soul. You are connected and your relationship to everything around you benefits from your attention as it supports you as well.

Things May Get Bumpy

Opening your heart and calling in your light can bring up many things. You may feel scared or anxious. You may even feel angry. Clearing your old stuff out makes room for the new. Please know that anything that you feel is exactly what you need to work through and it's perfect. You are perfect in every way. Your heart energy is strong, and it will demand what you need. Honor your heart with extreme honesty. Ask your heart daily for pure acceptance of where you are and what you need. Many people suggest talking things out, and usually that just brings up the old baggage; the physical act of writing helps to distance you from trauma, regret, and loss. You may need to journal strong feelings or difficult situations. Writing it out helps you heal. You are resilient and your body knows how to heal. Your heart wants to be joyful and free. Give it permission.

Raising Your Vibration

Sound is a powerful way to bring in more light and live a life of love. Om is an ancient spiritual sound used in many traditions. It symbolizes the union of mind, body, and spirit. In the Hindu tradition, it contains the vibrations of creation. It is also used in yoga to mark the beginning of a special time and space for the practice and at the end to re-enter society. It sounds like two syllables when pronounced "ah-oo-mm," it can be grounding and connecting at the same time.

OM Exercise

Say Om. Your lips come together and sense the connection and completeness. Take another deep breath and say Om. Your throat vibrates. Feel it throughout your body. If it feels right, hum and let the vibration explore the channels in your body. Determine where the sound vibration expands, where it feels small. Play with the sound, the vibration, the sensations. Try closing your eyes to tune into your sensations. They are yours. Your energies when paired with intentions fuel your desires and clear areas to let in more of what you desire.

Here is your first devotion. Say to yourself or aloud.

Pure Acceptance Devotion

Dear Divine Source, Divinity, God, Goddess, Jesus, Soul Guides, or Loving Angels,

Help me calm my body and my mind. With every breath I invite space, room for my loving presence. With every exhalation I release the things that no longer serve me. As I release them, I thank them and smile. Now there is room for my love. I am ready to invite love. I feel it filling the space I created. My touch is beautiful, and my caress is sweet. My body reacts to my touch, and it is safe. It is safe to feel my pleasure. My pleasure is good. I accept any emotions I feel and honor them. I give myself permission to laugh, squeal, shake, moan, jump, sleep, purr, ache, yell, whisper, and vibrate. I am free. My feelings are pure perfection.

And so, it is.

Thank you. Thank you. Thank you.

Awareness Brings Clarity

You may have habits that pull you away from your divinity. Be mindful of what you are energizing. Your attention, focus, and energy are your power. Stop giving your power away to things that don't give back. People who give back to you are the ones who deserve your attention and loving power. Be aware of how you spend your time. It is your choice. When you have a moment do you check in on your beautiful body and the beautiful souls around you? You may be addicted to technology. If your attention is pulled by your phone or your computer and you find yourself distracted or irritated when you are away from your devices, you may be addicted. If walking away from your phone feels strange or causes you anxiety, you may be addicted. Your technology is there to improve your life. If it is dictating your life, it's time for a plan. The first step is awareness. Next, decide what notifications are important to you and which ones you can silence. Make sure you are in control of your attention, and you are using your technology to improve your life. Think of technology as a tool and not a security blanket. Be free.

Self-Care is the Foundation of Love

Self-care is crucial to your happiness and connecting to your light. You may have been programmed to think that being selfless makes you a better person, and that putting others' needs before yours makes you caring and important. This view has some challenges. First of all, if you neglect your needs to care for someone else consistently, you are going to burn out. Also, if you are giving without feeling and in total service, your gift is shallow and less meaningful. To love and experience sensuality on any level, you must be in a good place. You are showing up for another person not just because it's expected, but because you wish to share your gifts with them. These gifts come without thinking. They come from a place of complete presence and your loving instinct. Your gifts are precious and special. People are privileged to receive them.

Once your basic needs are met, you can have compassion and care for others. There will be less distraction because you can be present knowing that your basic needs are met. The idea that you should put yourself second only leads to more imbalance. Those around you will feel when you are stretched; just as they will feel when you are calm and happy. Rushing around trying to make everything perfect and others happy is an exercise in delusion. Tuning into your needs will make you more efficient in tuning into the real needs of those around you. For example, you may think that doing the laundry and having everything folded precisely is important to show your family you care. However, if you feel isolated and taken for granted when you do laundry, it's a chance to tune into your feelings and shift the dynamic. Start with honest self-reflection. Ask yourself, "Where are these feelings coming from? Are there facts that I can relate to share my experience?"

Pillars of Health

When feeling a bit out of sorts, come back to the basics. You can't soar with joy until your body, your temple, is cared for.

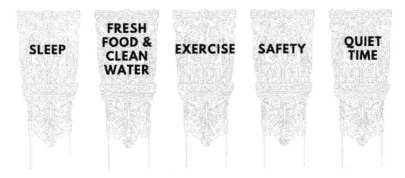

| SLEEP | FRESH FOOD & CLEAN WATER | EXERCISE | SAFETY | QUIET TIME |

SLEEP: The average woman needs 9 hours of sleep. Your body and mind heal and process information in your sleep.

FRESH FOOD & CLEAN WATER: If you can't find fresh foods, buy frozen. Your nutrition is the fuel your body needs to function optimally. Think quality over quantity.

EXERCISE: Your body needs movement to work through stress, problem solve, and remove toxins.

SAFETY: Anxiety is increased if you feel threatened or unsafe. Find ways to empower your sense of safety. Take a self defense class. Have a plan.

QUIET TIME: Peace and quiet are essential to your joy and sensuality. Find ways to spend 5-10 minutes in peace and quiet.

Share with them, "I would really like help with the laundry so that I have more time to do things with you." Ask them what they would like to do with you. Maybe your child would really like you to read a book to them or play a game with them. Tell them things that make you happy. When you are rested, calm, and happy it's easy to see what needs to be changed. You can create any dynamic you want when you are present and aware, and you can be more efficient with your time.

Message from the Angels for Self-Care

Dear One,

We love, love, love you. You do not have to prove anything to be loved. You are on earth to love yourself first, then when your cup is full, love others and show them how to love you back. You make it difficult sometimes, but really all you need to do is ask. People around you want to love you, care for you, and protect you. Being vulnerable gives others a chance to stand up and protect you. Every experience good and bad has a function. Good is easy. Challenging experiences are there to show you how to love, forgive, stand up, rest, and move on. Your dear soul wants to show you many things. Be still and you will hear its messages. They can be comforting and reassuring. Your soul can reveal how unwanted things can transform into something more beautiful than you ever dreamed. You must trust, my dear. Follow your heart and listen to your body's cries for it needs to be nurtured for you to have bliss. Your bliss will change the world.

Two-Minute Self-Care Routine

When you only have a couple minutes, choose one or two of these:

- Close your eyes and breathe deeply.

- Drink a glass of water.

- Take a deep breath, stretch your arms over your head, and breathe out. Then bring them down. Rotate your neck slowly in one direction, and then in the other. Shrug your shoulders up and rotate them back.

- Massage the pressure points on your neck just below your earlobes. The easiest way to find them is to put your fingers behind your ear about halfway down. Follow the curve of your ear to just behind the earlobe where your jaw and your neck meet. Touch and massage that area. When you feel the tender spot, you are on it! It can be intense to apply light pressure to this area, so do what feels best to you. Relax and breathe.

- Dab your favorite essential oil on your temples or neck.

Essential Oils Use

Essential oils carry the specific energy of plants in a concentrated way. Using them can help you direct and flow voltage in a positive direction for your needs. Lavender and peppermint are some of the most versatile essential oils; think lavender to calm and relax and peppermint to invigorate. Here are some common symptoms and the oils that can help:

Agitation: lavender, orange, roman chamomile, vetiver, ocotea

Mental fatigue: frankincense, black pepper, sage, peppermint

General fatigue: lemongrass, basil, lemon, rosemary, thyme, peppermint

Headache: tangerine, jasmine, geranium, frankincense, peppermint, lavender, Roman chamomile

Five-Minute Self-Care Routine

Choose one or two of these when you only have five minutes or less to rebalance:

- Make a cup of tea. While the water is heating, complete any of the activities from the Two Minute Self-Care Routine.

- Take a quick walk.

- Pet or talk to an animal.

- Gaze out the window.

- Listen to meditation music at 528Hz. This frequency is proven to be healing. Many music streaming services have playlists tuned to 528Hz.

- Place a cool washcloth on your face. Just breathe.

Thirty-Minute Self-Care Routine

Choose one of these when you can spend at least thirty minutes:

- Make a bath and soak in Epsom salts. Add a few drops of neutral oil such as almond, grapeseed, or liquid coconut and a few drops of essential oil. My favorites are lavender, peppermint, palo santo, geranium, and bergamot.

- Take a shower; let the water carry away anything that no longer serves you.

- Exercise: a good sweat detoxes the body and clears the mind.

- Take time to connect with yourself spiritually: pray or meditate.

- Set a thirty-minute timer. Lie down. Get comfortable. If you have trouble getting cozy, tense up your muscles and then starting from your head relax each body part down to your toes by breathing and telling each part to let go. Take a nap or just lay quietly.

- Make a smoothie or a fresh snack. Ask the food to rejuvenate and provide you ultimate health.

- Call a friend.

Presence Exercise

Take a deep breath. Breathe into peace and gratitude. In your grateful heart you are open. With each breath you are more open to receiving the light. It shines on you. You pick the color as it transmits through your body down from your head and swirls to your toes. It's an infinity loop traveling in a swirling motion from your toes and below and then back up to your crown and down. You receive this light, as it is your divine right. The calm, centered joy you feel in your heart when you are connected is your soul presence. You are timeless and precious.

Message from the Angels about Helping You

Dear One,

We are pleased to contact you. We feel your struggle and want to help lighten your burden. We will be here to guide you on your journey. We are here to help you find your mystery, your curiosity, and your joy. Connecting to your mystery involves letting go of expectations of all kinds and being totally present in the moment. Stop and feel what's happening around you, inside you, and notice the nature around you: the buzzes, the calling, the birds singing, or quiet people encouraging each other or maybe discouraging. The moments you connect with your surroundings are the moments you feel most alive, and you feel the most centered. You can send loving energy to anything within your attention. If you have a pet, you may experience this readily. Babies tend to react to this loving attention as well. You are one. Love is all around you.

Thank you.

Living at a High Frequency

People may not understand if you come with a high vibration, and they may try to bring you down to their level. You may have used drugs or alcohol to come down to their level as well. Depressants can calm the frequencies and muffle your dimensions. Sometimes it's easier to hide or mask your true light because it is different. Shining through and being true to your fears and realizing that you are different takes real courage. Once you embrace your uniqueness, you are free from those fears. You honor your unique reason for being here. The fear of rejection is completely conquered once you face it because you are living your truth. I love sheep, but I want you to know that people are not here on this great planet to act like sheeple. We are here to grow, express, create, explore, and find our unique joy.

Invitation and Intent Devotion

Dear Divine Source, Divinity, God, Goddess, Jesus, Soul Guides, or Loving Angels,

I am asking for your help. I invite your healing and loving presence into my life. I may not see every sign, so please use your invention to reach me. I will look for repeating numbers to remind me of love and abundance. I will notice songs or tunes that repeat, birds visiting me, flowers swaying in my direction, feathers, sweet air, the breeze, the cleansing effect of water, sudden goosebumps or chills and many other ways you reach out to me. I will try to quiet my mind to take in subtle hints or thunderbolts of information that are so loud I cannot ignore them. I realize that repeating events, words, and dreams are ways you try to reach me. I am open to getting the messages because I know you are sending them to help me in your loving way. Please send people for my highest good to help me on my way so that my soul purpose can radiate. I welcome clarity to raise my frequency for the betterment of myself and therefore all life around me.

Thank you. Thank you. Thank you.

Disruption Leads to Change

I want you to know that sometimes it will feel challenging. And that's okay! No change is made without a disruption. Even positive changes can be disruptive. Even though you know it's not serving you, your old paradigm can be comfortable and familiar. It's okay. Accepting yourself can be messy. You may need to break through barriers and your past unconscious choices. Listen to what you need. Listen to your body. You may need to scream, hide, run, rant, journal, sing, moan, soak, eat, fast, pray, talk, question, argue, disagree, or maybe, just sit in silence. Tune into yourself. What do you feel? It's there for a reason. Don't you love that? Communicate to those close to you about things you are working through and explain that you may seem distracted or behave differently. They may have questions or look for ways to support you. Healing support will show up for you.

Divine Cleansing Oxygen Devotion

Dear Divine Source, Divinity, God, Goddess, Jesus, Soul Guides, or Loving Angels,

Please help me quiet my mind. Draw in my breath deeply, filling my lungs with potential of renewal and light. Exhale out the old and stale. Inhale light and love. Exhale what no longer serves me. Help me be present with each system in my body. Invite the breath to go into areas of congestion or tension. Send healing love to those areas. Bring me the information I need to heal and for my body to repair. I know I have the power to heal as I connect to unconditional love and acceptance. I breathe in healing. I am health. The answers are near.

With gratitude,

Thank you. Thank you. Thank you.

It's optional but if you feel like making a sound here, you can end the devotion with a loving tone such as a low AHHHH, OOOOOH, NEWWWWW. A High-pitched AHHHHHHHH sounds help you connect with your source and bring you joy.

Chapter 2

Finding Your Release

What brings you joy? Find the repetitive activity you can do that clears you and clarifies your being. Some people jog, bike, lift weights, listen to music, dance, meditate, walk, paint, color, knit, drive, shop, write, sing, bird watch, garden, clean, get a massage, acupuncture, or any other activity. When thoughts come up, honor them. The thoughts that surface during repetitive activities are clues for you. Know that any fear, worry, or doubts that surface during these repetitive activities are needed. Feel these, make friends with them. Ask yourself if they need to be a part of your story or if you are ready to release them.

Honesty with Difficult Emotions Can Lead to Joy

Fear, doubt, and worry are powerful emotions that can pave your way to joy. Think of them as levels you have to pass through to get to the bonus round. Joy cannot be present with them, nor can you simply ignore them or step past them. Honestly facing your fears, doubts, and worries and owning your uniqueness is not easy. It takes courage to be present with fears and doubts. Be honest with yourself. Really feel what is happening; greet your emotion with curiosity. For example, you can say, "Hello anxiety, what's up?" and then take a deep cleansing breath and become aware of your shoulders. Shrug them up and let them go as you breathe out. Your shoulders take on so much

15

tension, it may feel good to repeat this several times until you feel the muscles release. Taking deep breaths tells your old reptilian brain, the part which is there to help you survive bear attacks and floods, that you are okay. The perceived danger is now extinct. Grab a piece of paper. Write down what is not true about that unwanted feeling. Now take a deep breath. You see, simply breathing and recognizing what is not true about that feeling helps you clear it and move on. Now tell yourself what is true. "I am safe; I am protected; I am living with courage." Pushing things away and pretending they don't exist only gives unwanted feelings more power.

Sometimes you just have to talk it out. The number one rule is to only mention fears and doubts to others if you have a solution. For example, if you are scared that your partner is going to get into a car crash, explore where that fear is coming from. Is it fear of being alone, abandonment, or simply driving? I get it! My husband drives in Atlanta daily and the fear is real on the highways! You could talk to your partner about your fear and see if they would text or call you when they arrive at work. Or maybe that's a special time for the two of you to talk while they are driving in?

Accept that unwanted feelings are just as important as those feelings you desire. In embracing all your emotions, you move away from duality and into wholeness. Letting the entire range of feelings and emotions run through you is part of mastering your sensuality. You can take the feeling and recognize that it is fuel for connecting more deeply. Be honest with yourself. The sooner you face the unknown of the cave of unwanted emotions, the less control it will have over you. I believe that repression of any feelings and the burying of base emotions lead to anger, violence, and abuse. You must let that power run through you. Everything you think and feel has a pulse and projection out into the field. We need to give and take to maintain a healthy flow. It is essential to accept all that we feel and then release it. Keeping it in can lead to serious blockages.

You Decide

We are living on a planet that has evolved. It's time to tell our brains it's okay to function with a new set of rules. The only way to do that is to breathe and let your heart send the message of comfort and connection to Source. Have gratitude for your complex being. You make the rules, and you are in control of how you spin your story. In every moment, you get to decide. You are responsible for your health, wealth, happiness, and freedom because only you can define them. This is not to blame you for your hurt, this is to understand people go through this. Through self-discovery and self-care, you will find joy on the other side.

New Beginnings Devotion

Dear Divine Source, Divinity, God, Goddess, Jesus, Soul Guides, or Loving Angels,

Please help me move out of my old ways of thinking and being which no longer serve me. Bring me the patience and self-love I need to spend time doing what brings me joy. I know that I can work through my old ways and move out of my old patterns using repetitive movements and new thinking. I feel your presence and support as I confront my fears; I breathe and honor my fears because they once served me. Now I can let them go.

With gratitude,

Thank you. Thank you. Thank you.

Abundance and Freedom in Your Uniqueness

In the past, society was survival-based. We needed to compete for resources to survive. Part of surviving was fitting in and playing your role. Now, we have plenty of resources, we just have to stop hoarding them. Everyone on this planet has a contribution to make. Look at the children around you. They are not concerned about fitting in or playing roles. They have picked up on the shift. When you find your soul's purpose for being here, you find peace and contentment. It's easy to follow the herd and do what you are told: Buy the same handbag as your friends, have the same haircut, or drive the same car. This mindless following allows you to blame someone else if things go wrong. Excuses like, "I was just following orders" or "Everyone is doing it" seem acceptable or frankly just easier than thinking independently. How many sad things have happened in our world because the people were just blindly following orders?

You are better than that. You can make choices and decide what is best for you. Because you love yourself, you will want to protect what matters to you. You want to be happy. You want to be healthy, and you care about your world. You see, loving yourself connects you deeply to this life and builds connections to others. The answer is not in the collective good. The answer is in the individual good. As each person is valued, our world is healed. Healing can never take place when the individual is not seen or respected. This is not something one person can tell another person. It is not reached by comparing or competing. It is something each person defines for themselves. You cannot give this power away; it is yours. Your power. Each person is a unique piece of the puzzle. That is the challenge. Your true happiness and health are not determined by someone else. They are your responsibility. Your goal is to find and explore your needs and then celebrate how the world benefits from your love and joy. That is true happiness and satisfaction. The scary thing is that it's up to you. You may feel exposed or vulnerable but those are signs that you are on the right track. Think of yourself as an explorer, finding new frontiers in yourself. No one else can tell you what it looks like in your life. It's an absolute self-discovery only found in the quiet spaces in your sovereign soul.

The Path to Joy Devotion

Dear Divine Source, Divinity, God, Goddess, Jesus, Soul Guides, or Loving Angels,

Help me live in the present and be open to the mysteries and miracles around me. From the sweet smell of the flowers to the crunch of a crisp, sweet apple, let me experience the sensations around me as an innocent child. When I am present, I discern things I wish to avoid. I forgive myself and release guilt and shame now. Help me release habits and addictions that no longer serve me and step into what resonates with me. I can tell what I need by what brings me joy. It fills me up and makes me strong. Help me to be open to joy and realize that it has no limits.

I am joy. Joy I am.

Thank you. Thank you. Thank you.

Making Space for the New

There are signs you need to clear your body of old baggage. You may feel tired, burnt out, uninspired, bored, or disinterested. The best way to release these states is to move. Get out and move; shake them away. These feelings are low vibrations, and they won't serve your loving soul. Another powerful way to release your feelings and frustrations is to write them out with pen and paper. It doesn't have to make sense.

You could draw pictures to represent your troubles. One time I just made big lines with a super jumbo Sharpie until I felt a shift in my heart. Or maybe it was the smell of the marker getting to me! Just kidding. The goal is not to relive the difficulties but to make them objective. This will give you perspective, and then you can let them go. You may feel yourself going back to the same issues and that's normal. Just keep writing or drawing. Your heart wants to heal. Then dispose of the papers. I like to burn them and watch the smoke filter up and away. My baggage is released into the universe.

Emotions Can Create a Mindset

Dragging old emotions or buried feelings out into the light is messy stuff. There are many approaches and many ways to clear this out. Please know when you feel scared or desperate, it's completely normal. Do not fight it or bury it deep inside. You need to honor these feelings. Own them. You can say something like, "I am so scared of being hurt but this time I want to release the fear and try." Sit with that. Take a deep breath. Do you feel hurt now? Your mind creates your reality. Have you considered that pain can be a condition or a mindset? You can create pain by fabricating a situation that hasn't even happened.

Think about the last time you got a shot. If you told yourself, "This is going to hurt; this is going to hurt," your muscles tensed up, you anticipated pain. Your brain then waited for the validation: Yes, there's the needle; it's going in and it's hurting. Many people make a face before the needle even goes in! What if you took a deep breath, stayed calm, and relaxed? The needle would have less resistance with your muscles relaxed and your arm would be less sore after. Maybe it really hurt last time, but that is over. Who knows what this time is going to be like? Wouldn't it be better to have a fresh start? Why add the pain from the last shot to this one? The same applies to any situation in your life where you may be experiencing physical, spiritual, emotional, or mental pain. What do you need to release? What part of the story is no longer true?

Freedom in Grace Devotion

Dear Divine Source, Divinity, God, Goddess, Jesus, Soul Guides, or Loving Angels,

I request grace. Please help me think about myself with grace and give those around me pure grace. I know that snapping to quick judgments or assumptions robs me of precious moments. I realize that my harshness and judgments about myself take me away from a divine state of grace. Help me see when I am responding with a lack of grace or when I am responding out of fear, worry, or doubt. When I do so, I pay a price. That price is hope and belief. Help my belief and hope flourish by finding grace and neutrality. I realize it's a practice and I won't be perfect but please show me the positive results of my efforts in the miracles around me. Each moment is a chance for change. I am alive and given each day to create the reality I desire.

I just need to ask.

And so, it is.

FEAR: False Evidence Appearing as Real

Fears are the ultimate baggage. Our brains try to protect us but in reality, being scared and staying scared makes you easy to control and takes your resources away. Fear has been used to manipulate others. Wouldn't it be better to take the feeling and build knowledge or awareness? For example, many people are scared of drowning. It is a very real fear for a good reason. If you can't swim you will drown and die. That's scary! Parents want to protect their children, so either they keep their children away from water, or they teach them to swim. They empower that child to move their arms and legs and learn how to navigate the water and how to respect the water. Boom! Fear is gone and new skills are learned. What if we faced all fear like children when they learn to swim? Focus our big, dewy, trusting eyes on our teacher, jump in, and keep moving. You've got this! You just have to see your fears, honor them, and find the right teachers or resources so you can build knowledge and trust in the process. When you feel fear, try to find the facts and trust your instincts.

Fear Can Hold You Back

Here's another example. You may have been really burned by trusting and loving someone with all your heart. Now you withhold parts of your heart and pieces of your soul to protect yourself from hurt. In every relationship you look for ways the other person can let you down. And you end up saying to yourself, "See this is what I thought would happen. I knew it was going to hurt." Is that fair? Why give the person who hurt you the first time (or the last time) power over that part of you that makes you most connected and can bring you so much joy?

Being Brave and Honest

Please know that you may see patterns reoccurring, and if so, it's your chance to learn from them. Are you sticking up for your feelings and communicating with honesty? You don't have to be a doormat for love. Stand strong for what you need, and if that person isn't strong enough or available for you, it's okay. Has the relationship run its course? It may hurt, but you can use this to explore what you consider ideal. You can't control how others love you, but you can ask for what you want. Someone worth your attention will try. Sharing often about what you like makes the other person more open to sharing what they would like. Your vulnerabilities, believe it or not, can be sexy or even free up your partner to share their own. This brings more joy to your relationship and draws you to be closer to each other or shows you that it may not be the right place for you. Either way you learn about your loving soul and honoring the needs of your lover. Being scared of losing something and holding on to it harder doesn't bring it closer to you. Focus on the love, not the loss. As author Spencer Johnson reminds us, "Every moment is a gift. That's why they call it the present." Your ability to feel love is related to how you can show love. It's a mirror and the more you see love in yourself, the more you will recognize love around you.

Emotional Freedom Devotion

Dear Divine Source, Divinity, God, Goddess, Jesus, Soul Guides, or Loving Angels,

Please help me release old fear and hurt. Dissolve the connections of past relationships and anything in present relationships that keep me from loving completely. I realize past experiences can affect my happiness now, and I choose to release the past so I can live in my present. Let me feel the flow of releasing those stuck places and fill them with light and hope. Let me be open to my joy and the gifts around me. Open my awareness to love in all things and let me shine love to others.

Thank you. Thank you. Thank you.

Chapter 3

Surroundings Set the Mood

What is around you? Do you have things around you that bring you joy? What is in your home that makes you happy? Are there spaces you avoid where you stash things you aren't ready to deal with? Here's the thing, this is a metaphor for your life. You have to get in the corners and get them cleared out to have clarity and peace. You need space, air, and light to feel free and bring in your highest expression.

Simplicity Brings Peace

Although many people get a sense of peace and joy from a place of minimalism, some people get a sense of security from the things around them. Look around you. Consider if your stuff could be weighing you down. Not just physically, but financially as well. Excess can cause stress. Do you have debt associated with the clutter around you? Part of living a life of love is releasing that which no longer serves you. If you are spending all your time working to pay off things, you don't have time to enjoy them. You are simply working for the idea of joy.

In the next chapter we will explore your Joy List. We'll also focus on your core values a little later in this chapter. Knowing them will help you decide about what to keep in your life and what needs to be released for your freedom. Question your possessions and determine if they improve your life or if they are simply things you have. Exercise your freedom to choose, before you buy something, consider if it brings you function and joy. Remember, you will leave this world as you came in, with absolutely nothing. Your life. Your choice.

Declutter

Start with your bedroom. Tackle the closet and under the bed. Check your closet. Do you have some things in there simply collecting dust? Maybe some items are sentimental. It's time to thank them and let them go. They once provided warmth and joy to you. Now they may need to be released so that someone else may use them. You need space for your new life of love.

Control Your Surroundings

Surround yourself with textures, scents, and sounds that make you feel good. Pay attention to clothing. Things you haven't worn in over twelve months are simply cluttering your life or taking up space you could use for something functional to you. Go through your clothing. Every item you wear should be comfortable and make you feel good. The clothing and the colors you wear represent your confidence and mindset. If something fits strange, or makes you uncomfortable in any way, it's time to let it go. After acknowledging its special memory or purpose, pass on the items which no longer serve you. Donate them to charity if you like or even look into reselling them.

Now that you have decluttered and opened space, enjoy it. Place the intention that your space is special and a sanctuary from the outside world. Feel free to bless your home anytime you like. Some like to clear energy at every new moon for a fresh start.

Elements to Consider Creating Balance and Harmony in Your Home

Elements In Your Home

Incorporating elements with intention can enhance your space, bring clarity, and promote peace in your surroundings.
May everything you gaze upon be blessed with peace and grace.

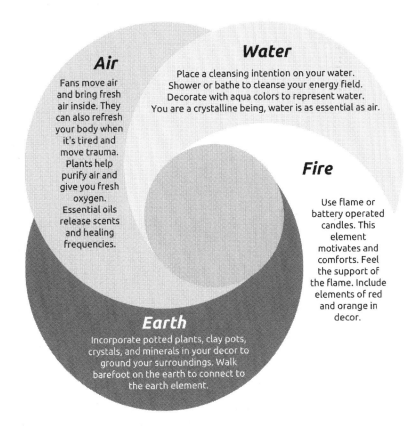

Air
Fans move air and bring fresh air inside. They can also refresh your body when it's tired and move trauma. Plants help purify air and give you fresh oxygen. Essential oils release scents and healing frequencies.

Water
Place a cleansing intention on your water. Shower or bathe to cleanse your energy field. Decorate with aqua colors to represent water. You are a crystalline being, water is as essential as air.

Fire
Use flame or battery operated candles. This element motivates and comforts. Feel the support of the flame. Include elements of red and orange in decor.

Earth
Incorporate potted plants, clay pots, crystals, and minerals in your decor to ground your surroundings. Walk barefoot on the earth to connect to the earth element.

Sacred Space Devotion

Dear Divine Source, Divinity, God, Goddess, Jesus, Soul Guides, or Loving Angels,

Bring in light and love to my space. Place columns of light at the four corners of my home. From the columns let them radiate your love and peace with a halo of light. May my home be a place of sanctuary to all who enter. Cleanse my home from any energy of conflict or darkness and let there be only light and the supporting energy of love and acceptance.

And so it is, and so it is.

Thank you. Thank you. Thank you.

Think about what brings you most joy out of the elements: air, water, fire, and earth. This will help you know what to bring into your sacred space.

Your Surroundings Reflect Your Values

It is not just what you have in your home and how it's organized, it is also important to consider what you are bringing into your home energetically. What kind of entertainment are you drawn to? Do the things you give your attention to match the kind of life you want to live?

What's important to you? What do you want to keep in your life and what would you like to bring in? Take some time to visualize your perfect day. What are the five most important things in your life? If it helps, I have a list of some possibilities. There are no wrong answers.

VALUES

CIRCLE YOUR TOP FIVE

Connection	Truth
Abundance	Authenticity
Freedom	Love
Career	Empathy
Faith	Poise
Freedom	Beauty
Health	Autonomy
Leadership	Independence
Harmony	Wisdom
Compassion	Patience
Soul-Purpose	Creativity
Honesty	Community
Dedication	Service
Clarity	Recreation
Stability	Productivity
Balance	Caring
Strength	Flexibility
Exploration	Divinity
Trust	Growth
Grace	Peace
Learning	Curiosity
Joy	Knowledge
Grit	Intuition

It's up to you because you get to create the life you want. The first step is to identify your ideal life. Many times, we are so busy surviving and taking care of others, we overlook what is important to us. Take this time to deeply consider what you value, what you want to focus on today. This could change tomorrow, or it may stay the same. Your values will keep you grounded in your purpose and show the world what you are about.

Your life is your creation.

Think of how your values can drive and motivate your life. When you wander from your list you may feel a lack of joy or frustration. Living in your values can fuel your dreams. Do any of them spark deep feelings? Those feelings are clues. Sit with them and see if you can determine where those feelings came from. Have you been giving yourself the gift of these core values? When you live from them you create a better world just by being you.

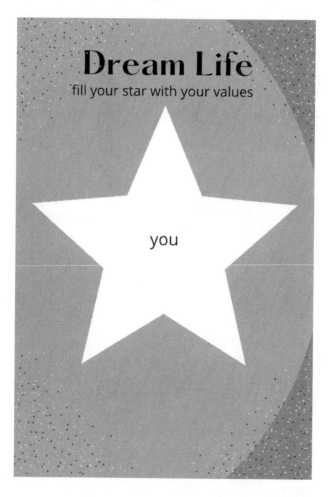

Values and Life Purpose Devotion

Dear Divine Source, Divinity, God, Goddess, Jesus, Soul Guides, or Loving Angels,

Open my heart so I may feel the rush of excitement when I am in my purpose, my true joy in filling the need that only I can fill. When I get quiet and ask from my heart, I can hear the answer. Even if I judge it, you will show me again and again for I can be stubborn and blind with my opinions. I yearn for the satisfaction of making my world exactly the way I envision with the highest good. Grant me clarity for my values because my beliefs will guide me to be true to myself. With honesty, I show the ultimate self-love. I am an amazing being of unlimited potential and divine design.

Thank you. Thank you. Thank you.

Nature Can Provide Clarity

You can reduce stress and improve your mood by spending time in nature. Searching for flowers, gazing at the sky, admiring trees, and listening to the birds are great ways to reduce stress and help you feel connected to the earth.

Part of being a human is feeling the density of the earth. The strong magnetic pull of your body and the earth's consciousness can be very draining. There will be times you will need to release the density and recharge. If you feel heavy, drained, or distracted, and things you usually do without effort seem taxing, you are absorbing the collective consciousness. This is normal but you can process it with an intention to clear it and reset. The first set is acknowledging the feelings. Ask your body how it is doing and really listen. It may surprise you. Take time to recharge and reset.

Grounding Exercise

With your shoes off, lie on your back with your knees bent and feet planted into the ground. As you breathe in, squeeze your butt muscles and abs so that your body rises up with your shoulders still planted on the earth. Your body will look like a ramp. Release your breath and lower your butt down to the ground. Repeat this motion at your own pace at least thirty times. As thoughts enter your mind, honor them and release them. Movement and breath can move tension out of your body and restore you. You may feel warmth as your body senses the movement. Play around with the tension as you squeeze and feel the strength in your muscles and your core. When you finish, place one hand, palm down on your heart and the other hand on your navel. This is where your power and perseverance come from. Honor your energy center of power and appreciate how it is affected by your movement and attention.

Connecting to My Divinity Devotion

Dear Divine Source, Divinity, God, Goddess, Jesus, Soul Guides, or Loving Angels,

Help me to step away from fear and into service. I realize that people around me are needing my attention and there are people who need to serve me too. We depend on each other. I know that I am an Earth Angel and my light is bright but can be brighter when I see each person around me as a Divine Soul. This loving energy is compounding and beautiful. Help me always realize the positive change available near me.

Amen.

Chapter 4

Room for Joy

There will be times you will struggle to find joy. This is normal. You are creating a blank slate, an empty page to decide what you want. Be creative. Be honest. Be curious. Also realize the power of intention for creating space for joy. Your days, your moments have been created by your experiences and your reactions to those moments. At some point, you prioritized someone or something else in the place of joy. Reclaim that space in your life for you. It's time to reclaim joy. Think of it as cleaning out a drawer. You bought something new, now it's time to make space for it by getting rid of something old which no longer serves you.

Clearing Out the Old Exercise

Find a quiet, dark space or just a quiet space where you can sit or lie down wearing a sleep mask. Before you make it dark read this passage:

Quiet in the dark. Can you tolerate the nothingness? Turn into it. Lean in and open to it until you feel the void fill in with warmth and power. Embrace what you are given. Your longing and searching manifests into a flow. The nothingness is now your new world created in the vision of your soul with flashes of light and peace. Nothingness connects you to your peace and your centered, most genuine self. From the nothingness you can visualize your supreme life, your light contribution.

Now set a five-minute timer and complete the exercise. Remember: no judgments.

Message from Archangel Michael about Your All-Knowing Soul

Dear One,

Please be calm. Settle your breath. In and out. You are one. In the calmness find your honesty. It's your core of how you feel. Trust in your random thoughts. Write them down, sing them out, whisper them, or scream them out into the universe. Acknowledge your dark thoughts as they are important and need to be honored. You matter. Honesty with yourself is power. You are a brave warrior for your truth. You are a loving vessel of manifestation. You are one. Say "I am love, love I am. I am love, love I am. I am love, love I am." Repeat it until your heart calms and a wave of peace flows over your being. This day is a gift, and each moment a new beginning.

Amen.

Attention Creates Thoughts and Reality

Everything starts with you and your awareness. First you sense the environment, and your brain determines how you focus your attention by selecting the stimuli of interest. Consider that your reality is simply what you are sensing and what your brain determines to be of interest. Your brain builds thoughts around what you sensed and noticed. This explains how two people can be in the same situation and each person can have a distinctly different reality. Our senses, then thoughts, create our reality. Change the way you think, and you change your reality. Feel and acknowledge your truth. Which sensations bring you the most pleasure? What would you like to change? Take the time to check in on yourself. What pleases you? The clearer you can be about what you want to experience, the better your brain can be recognizing those preferred experiences.

My Pleasures

Fill in your favorites

| Food |
| Animals |
| Movies |
| Art |
| Jokes |
| Vacations |
| Day of the Week |
| Colors |
| Types of Touch |
| Music |
| Nature |
| Books |
| Textures |

Authentic Joy Devotion

Dear Divine Source, Divinity, God, Goddess, Jesus, Soul Guides, or Loving Angels,

Open me to passion and flirty fun. Make me free from self-judgments and censorship so I can be authentic. In my authentic self, there is joy and power. I am willing to seduce and savor my passion by pushing and pulling my attraction with my eyes, my breath, my heart, and my hips. I love with my whole body and know that my love and passion are precious gifts to be given by me. The surrender comes with trust and knowing.

And so, it is.

Awareness Builds Joy

Take small moments to be aware. Step outside and feel the breeze on your skin and wisping through your hair. Let your nose absorb the fragrance of flowers. Enjoy the twinkle in a child's eyes as they explore the world. Be refreshed by cool water quenching your thirst. Be satisfied with the crunch of a crisp apple as you hold its perfection in your hand. Sink into the warmth of a cozy blanket. These moments are happening around you all the time. It's up to you to tune and be aware. You may claim that you don't have time, but time really seems to stop when you start to savor moments. You can still be productive while enjoying the moments. Simple tasks, such as washing a dish, can be sensual. You start with a very dirty dish. You command the streaming and pulsing warm water over your hands, as the foaming soap bubbles slip between your fingers, slipping, rubbing, and rinsing until that dish is squeaky clean and shining. Ha! I may need to go wash some dishes right now!

You have heard many people say, "Live in the moment." It's good advice. But I suggest not just living in the moment but saturating yourself in the moment. Time can stand still if you are open to the experiences around you at all times. There are symphonies in the background. Nature is calling you to notice. Animals and insects dare you to connect. There is so much around you. Once you start connecting to the subtle moments, everything and everyone will reflect back to you. You may sense a new clarity and awareness. You may start to sense when your dog needs something. You may feel it if your cat is looking at you. Your plants can suddenly thrive and grow to new heights. Life can slow down if you breathe and be present in the moments.

Action Step: Joy Exercise

Take a moment to look back at what you wrote in the My Pleasures chart. Each item can bring you joy. Pamper yourself with those things you can easily access today. Immerse yourself in the experience. Give yourself permission to feel pleasure and express gratitude.

Here's mine: I'm going to light a citrus candle, play yacht rock, and sit in my favorite chair, wearing my softest T-shirt and new socks. I'm going to wrap myself in a fluffy blanket, sip raspberry tea with honey, and watch the birds from my window. Your turn. Go!

Open to Joy Devotion

Dear Divine Source, Divinity, God, Goddess, Jesus, Soul Guides, or Loving Angels,

Please help me open up to true joy. I thank the fear and doubts that may be trying to protect me from feeling relaxed and happy. I no longer need this protection and I release it. It drifts away from me, and I replace it with a warm light which fills me and surrounds me. Light radiates from my being.

I am joy. Joy I am.

Without Joy, Things Can Get Boring

Bringing joy to relationships can be sticky after many years of being with someone. Our schedules can become repetitive. Although routines create predictability and stability, they can also lead to boredom. It's important to know how to bring and create joy in your relationships so they have new life and energy. I'd like to share the joy secret with you. It has to do with curiosity and openness.

The Joy Secret Exercise

Get quiet and breathe. Think about the last time you felt joy and a light heart. Maybe you can't think of the specific situation. If you have trouble visualizing it, make up what would be your idea of complete joy. Is it a litter of puppies on your lap with their fuzzy fur and pink noses nuzzling into you and surrounding you with their little whimpers? Maybe it's a perfect meal with a loved one. You may recall an achievement you worked hard for or a childhood memory. Is it a thousand kisses all over your body? Was it your last orgasm? What's your greatest fantasy? Is it baby goats jumping on a trampoline? Warm chocolate chip cookies? What makes it magical? Breathe into that experience and feel it in your heart. Many times, joy is involved in a novel experience. Maybe it's because you had curiosity and an open heart. Often this experience involved laughter or a deep inner peace. The secret is to live your life from one divine experience to the next. Look for ways to add curiosity to the mundane. Just being aware of any numb routines frees you up to invite renewal. Set a standard to focus on joy. If you routinely connect to curiosity and admiration, you have tapped into the joy secret.

Joy Cleanse Devotion

Dear Divine Source, Divinity, God, Goddess, Jesus, Soul Guides, or Loving Angels,

Help me remember true joy and how it lifts my heart and soul and lightens my load. Dissolve any connections or bonds that deplete my joy, washing them away with the wind and taking them to be transmuted into loving energy to feed more joy. Let me move with lightness and clarity. Help me choose joy and be one with this state upon my seeking and yearning. Let my joy be witnessed and emulated to spread more love and kindness into the world.

I am joy. Joy I am.

Thank you. Thank you. Thank you.

Take an Inventory of Your Time

Perhaps you are feeling overwhelmed by all the tasks in your life. Being in touch with frustration or exhaustion will guide you to your answers. You may be so busy checking things off your list that you overlook the resources you have. Stop for a moment and check in with your body. If your heart is racing and you feel rushed or stressed, chances are that you haven't had much time to enjoy anything from the My Pleasures chart you completed earlier in this chapter.

Can you prioritize what needs to be done instead of what you are doing simply out of habit? Maybe there are people around you who can help. Could your life be better organized by setting up playdates for your kids, asking for someone to help you run errands, maybe joining a carpool? Is it possible to have your groceries delivered and teach your kids how to help put things away? Invite others in your household to help with daily chores to help free up some of your precious time. You can start by making a list of everything you do for a week. It's easy to dictate it into a phone or jot it down on a piece of paper. What tasks can be delegated to others? From a peaceful heart, tell them that you would really like their help. Tell them how nice it would feel to work together as a team to make the house happy and how if everyone helped you would have more time to do fun things together. Explain how you have felt overwhelmed by all the things that need to be done. Then share your weekly task list with them. It will help them see all the things you do on a regular basis.

Ask your family if they are open to helping. If they say no, it's best not to react strongly. Stay calm and tell them it would mean a lot to you if they could find it in their hearts to help; encourage them to pick one or two things. I'm sure it's a long list and there will be something small they can start with. When they help, it may not be done exactly the way you would have done it, but please overlook that and have a gracious heart to say, "You made my day and I love that you emptied the dishwasher!" "Who folded all that laundry? You rock!"

Celebrating your family's help brings more joy into your house and into your world.

Embrace the Feelings Devotion

Dear Divine Source, Divinity, God, Goddess, Jesus, Soul Guides, or Loving Angels,

Help me to be open to all my emotions. They are unique and special to me. Each one tells me so much about what I need. None of them deserve to be pushed aside, ignored, or judged. I feel many uncomfortable emotions. Many times, I can't even make sense of my feelings. Help me be at peace with each emotion and let it be. Help me share how I am feeling with an objective voice. I realize my emotions can affect those around me. Many times, sharing how I feel can reassure the people around me that they are not responsible for my feelings. Being honest helps them respond in a loving way. I realize they may choose to give me space and it will be good. I may ask for a hug, or I may ask for them to give me space. It is all perfect in design. I do not judge, I just observe. I no longer withhold how I feel or mask it.

And so, it is.

Many of us nurture and like to please others. Pleasing someone and seeing their joy is fulfilling and often validating. Set an intention to allow others to nurture and please you. I get it. This may be very awkward and may require a paradigm shift. It may be a situation of role reversal. It's okay if it feels a little uncomfortable at first; that is perfectly normal.

Consider that by letting others care for you, you are sharing more love with them. I believe that the world works on give and take. So, if you are always giving, you are upsetting the balance of the world. You need to receive it as well. Also, your acts of self-love and requesting help open up a world of opportunity for those around you to feel fulfilled and validated—by seeing you feeling pleased and joyful they will also experience joy. Ultimately, it's selfish to not ask for help. Thanking those around you for showing up for you opens you up to the world of gratitude as it shows them that they can create positive change. You can help them become agents of joy and show them how to live a life of love.

Here's the secret. Really be present with your joy and let others know you are pleased. "It's so nice that you called me when you had a break. I was thinking about you too," or "Wow, I really like it when I have all your attention; it feels so good."

True joy is available when you feel most alive and free. Fear tends to make people give over their freedom and power to others for security. You need to feel alive and free to let in divine happiness. This happiness isn't purchased or won over. It's about living in your complete and balanced soul, in which you have freedom to follow your joy. Many people are worried about what tomorrow brings. In that state of worry and fear they are not free to be happy.

Knowing Myself Devotion

Dear Divine Source, Divinity, God, Goddess, Jesus, Soul Guides, or Loving Angels,

In my content heart, please fill me with respect for my total being. Provide me the patience to be kind to myself and gentle with my feelings and thoughts. Give me the peace to understand every one of my thoughts and feelings has worth and purpose. Help me to thank the doubts and use them to move forward with resolve and love to transform life. Help me to connect with my knowledge and strength and have courage to move in the direction of self-love and healing. And so, it is.

Thank you. Thank you. Thank you.

Action Step: Visualize Your Joy and Make a Joy List

In order to get what you want, you need to know what you want. How do you want to be loved? Spend some time thinking about how you would like to be treated by your partner and your loved ones. Really think about what is important to you and see it clearly. Imagine how it would feel, taste, and sound to have these moments of joy. With your thoughts you can create a new reality. Embrace the empowerment to define what pure joy means in a relationship. You can ask the Angels of Love to help you manifest what you want or something better. They love helping!

How do you share joy and what can others do for you?

JOY LIST

Circle the things that resonate with you or add your own

THINGS MY PARTNER COULD DO	WHAT MY FAMILY OR FRIENDS COULD DO
Light a candle	Hug me
Gaze in my eyes	Help make dinner
Rub my feet	Leave me a note
Hold my hand	Tell me how they feel
Dance with me	Tell me about their day
Look at the stars with me	Make me a cup of tea
Tell me the things that make me special	Sit with me
Confide in me	Fold the laundry
Share their dreams with me	Keep things tidy
	Share joyful times with me

THINGS I COULD DO

Smile: say hello	Enjoy my day
Be kind to old people	Recycle
Hold the door	Ask if I can help
Visit parks	Take care of nature
Know my neighbors	Pick up litter
Give grace	Thank a police officer
Buy local	Plant a tree
Listen	Find joy

Request for Joy

Dear Angels of Love and Relationships,

Help me visualize or feel perfect balance and satisfaction in my relationships. Bring my perfect match of joy and energetic connection. Help me see when my relationships reflect the ultimate joy of my desire or something even better for the highest good of all parties.

Thank you. Thank you. Thank you.

PART TWO

Loving Your Body

Chapter 5

Health is Giving Your Body Permission to Thrive

You deserve to live a full and vital life. You have seen her, a woman in the second half of her life who has more energy and spunk than someone half her age. What's her secret? How do her eyes sparkle like that? In contrast, there are people in their twenties with grey skin and an apparent apathy for life. It seems like every step is made with trepidation and effort. No doubt you can guess which woman is having more joy and passion in her life! Eating well can make all the difference. It's not complicated but it does take planning and mindfulness.

Food is a Prerequisite for Self-Care

Food is an important way to connect with the world around us. Consider the wonderful meals and the amazing culture we share through food. Food brings us together and nurtures us. We prepare and show we care through our meals and time we spend together eating. Foods also connect us to the earth. Nourishment comes from food that has captured wonderful energy from the sun in flavorful packages of potential energy for us to use as fuel and healing. Whole, fresh foods can be simply amazing sources of vitality.

Food Can Bring Vitality

A vital life of love is not about your body shape or the number on the scale. It's about being healthy and making the choices your body needs. It's about having a clear mind and an open perspective. You can take on what life throws at you because you have the fuel and the mindset to find love in situations and see the situation as it is. Your ego doesn't need to protect you because you are satisfied and clear.

Ignore the Headlines and Follow Your Body's Lead

Every day there is a new headline or diet book coming out. Diets can be centered in hype, trends to reach a target weight, or a short-term goal. The diet instructs you on how to focus on getting to the goal, but in reality, shouldn't the goal be to look and feel your best? Trends come and go, but a healthy lifestyle takes constant attention. Showing up as your most vital self is a lifelong practice of constantly choosing foods that resonate with your body and give you clean energy. What you eat helps your cells stay protected, gives you energy, and sets you up for success. To me that is not a diet; it's conscious living. A diet is a type of prescription. It may work for someone else, but you are an individual, your body has specific needs. A life of love involves doing what's best for your body. It also involves making loving food choices for your wellbeing—food choices that honor your health and show your pride.

The Calorie Game

All calories are not the same. A calorie is a unit of energy, but I would like to propose that the energy you get from eating a date is much different from the energy you get from a handful of chips. They may each have forty calories, but the date has vitamins, minerals, carbohydrates, antioxidants, and fiber while the chips have sodium, carbohydrates, no fiber, and fat from oils. The chips weigh you down, while the date sustains and supports your health. Find out nutritional information about your daily choices and use it to reinforce or make changes where you see opportunities for better choices. Consider this: The quality of the foods you eat matter more than the quantity.

Clean Eating Fuels a Loving Heart and Energetic Body

Your vitality directly affects all your relationships. There is no way you can be there for someone else if your body is trying to discern what the heck you are feeding it. Look at the ingredient labels on your foods. If there are things listed and you have no idea what they are, your body is not going to recognize those things either. It has to treat additives, preservatives, and pesticides as foreign substances and separate them from your vital organs. Oftentimes belly fat is a result of the body binding toxins (additives, preservatives, pesticides) from your food to a fat cell and moving them away from your vital organs. Your body wants to protect you and will change in order to do it! Your body doesn't care that you now have a muffin top over your belt; it just protects you from the invasions of additives and chemicals. In contrast, clean eating has a strong relationship to better blood flow and healthy blood pressure. People who eat organic, non-GMOs, while avoiding pesticides, added fats, and vegetable oils experience better health and optimal weight. They tend to have flatter stomachs and less jiggly thighs too.

Your body benefits from the clean energy from plants. They provide antioxidants, hydration, and carbohydrates without the fat and heavy digestive load of animal-based foods. When your blood is not laden with fat it can transport more oxygen to your muscles and brain. If you want to feel energy to do what pleases you, try to limit animal-based foods such as meats, eggs, dairy, and cheese, which raise the fat in your blood, tax your liver, and contribute to inflammation. Highly processed foods or fried foods can also tax your digestive system and put your body in an inflammation mode instead of the state you are looking for, which is optimal functioning mode. Highly processed foods are all full of calories and difficult to digest. If you can avoid processed foods, your thoughts will be clearer, your senses defined, and your energy will be used to fuel your day. Plants are not only lower in calories than processed foods (keep you trim), but plants can also help heal the inflammation you may have from stress or the environment.

More Flow = More Fun

Consider that the quality of what you eat can affect the performance of your body. Food additives and animal fats do not provide the clean energy required for optimal health and your highest love vibration. If you desire to live your life a different way, enjoy more loving, and feel more alive, the only place to start is with food choices. Consider that blood flow is critical for many bodily functions. Pleasure is associated with increased blood flow to sexual organs. Many people have experienced an increase sex drive and generalized satisfaction with their bodies when they switched to plant centered diets and limited animal fats. Do you want better orgasms and energetic workouts? You get them with better blood flow. Increasing your energy gives you more choices on how you can use that energy. Making love is a totally intense feeling when you have lots of clean energy at your disposal. The habit of eating mostly plants and meats that are raised and processed responsibly gives your body a chance to thrive and heal. Also staying away from fats and oils helps your body have more energy for getting things done.

As a Rule: Whole, Fresh Foods

Think fresh fruits and vegetables, whole grains, or beans with limited oils. When you have to use an oil, consider grapeseed oil and fresh pressed extra virgin olive oil. The habits of eating mostly plants and avoiding high sugar, fatty, and processed foods give your body a chance to thrive and heal. You know how you feel when you eat fried or heavy food? You crash and your body feels fried and heavy. When you choose a salad and whole grains over a cheeseburger, you can choose to use your energy. It may just mean more energy for getting busy. You can actually eat to have better sex.

The best foods for you are brightly colored. Walk in the produce aisle—or even better, the farmers market—what catches your eye? Really tune into what your eyes and stomach are telling you. Maybe you are a picky eater or grew up in a home without fresh foods. It's okay, you really can't mess this up. Be present and enjoy the cornucopia of options. Find a local farmers market, farming co-ops, or consider growing your own favorites. Fresh food can be affordable and delicious. You will be amazed at how much better a freshly picked fruit or home-grown vegetable tastes than one which has spent time in storage coolers and has been handled by multiple people. There is nothing like meeting the farmer who nurtured and grew the plant you are about to eat. You can sense their pride and you can see who you are supporting with your purchase. We are all connected and when you take the time to support those around you, you honor our interdependence.

The abundance of this earth will supply you with what you need. Consider the earth and you will be blessed with her abundance. Whatever you decide is okay, every person needs make their own choices. Be gentle with yourself in making changes. It's often a process. Your choices will be validated by your body responding with more ability to feel and show love. Treating your body as a precious flower and tending to it with honor will increase your ability to feel and give affection and care.

Healthy Food Choices Devotion

Dear Divine Source, Divinity, God, Goddess, Jesus, Soul Guides, or Loving Angels,

Please help me discover what foods support my health. Guide me to nutritious foods that satiate me, help my body detox, and build health. Please help me from craving foods which lead to imbalance in my body or habits that are hurting me. Help me to create resources to obtain the fresh foods I need and connect me to the farmers who grow foods with love and care. Help me to discern which foods will support me and which I should avoid. Raise my awareness of my body so that I can develop new habits and share my success with others who need help. In the name of the highest good, ultimate abundance, and respect for the earth and her creatures.

I am health. Health I am.

And so, it is.

Be Curious about Your Food

Living in love means consistently choosing what supports you. For example, discovering the foods that give you great energy and clarity and choosing them most of the time. If you have a weak moment and eat something that makes you feel less than great, be gracious. Don't beat yourself up, rather, make a mental note. Taking care of your body is the ultimate love you can show yourself. Consider what category a food would be by pausing before making a choice to see how it feels. A food is either positive, neutral, or negative. After you eat it, observe your body to see if your prediction matches how you feel. Then focus on eating foods that affect you positively. It's a process to find what works for you. As you practice defining if a choice is positive, negative, or neutral, you will gain confidence and strength in your choices.

Once you start to look at your choices you will find what's best for you. For example, eggs give me a headache, so they go in my negative category. I choose to get just as much protein from plants. One egg has 5 grams of protein, 5 grams of fat, and .6 grams of carbohydrates. One half cup of black beans has 2 grams more protein, 4.5 grams less fat, 19 grams more carbohydrates, and includes fiber which helps me stay full and reduces a blood sugar spike. Black beans are also full of other vitamins and nutrients which eggs lack. So really, I thank my body for having a reaction to eggs; it led me to make a better choice.

Here's another one. Ten years ago, I figured out through an elimination diet that chicken made me break out; I mean big, red neck acne! I talked to multiple doctors including my dermatologist, and none of them had ever heard of symptoms associated with chicken. Even though I knew I had to do it, giving up chicken was not easy. I am not kidding you when I say that I LOVE the taste of fried chicken. The peppery, crispy juiciness is still fresh in my mind and on my tongue. I live in the South and fried chicken is an art form here. I haven't eaten chicken in ten years. The feelings of brain fog, inflammation, and skin irritation are not worth it. Don't even get me started on the factory farming of meat. I'll just say, the mass production of chicken does not agree with my ethics or my skin! I choose to honor my body and avoid that which does not serve my highest good. Each person needs to make their own choices based on what they believe in and support.

Do Any Foods Affect You Negatively?

Take the time to really feel how food is affecting you. I infrequently eat beef and dairy because of the ways the animals are treated and the environmental consequences. The health risks are also just not worth it for me. I tend to feel better when I stick to a plant-based diet and have meat occasionally. I like to stay active. After eating a plant-based meal, I can enjoy a nice workout, or even an afternoon delight and not feel heavy or bloated. I no longer have to time my activities around my meals and digestion. Your diet and your choices are yours to make. Just tune into how you feel and see what works for you.

Hot, Red, or Puffy Skin is a Clue

Although you can often feel it when you eat something that is not optimal for you, your skin can also give you clues. There are foods known to cause inflammation. The worst offenders are sugar, artificial colors, flavors, processed flour, gluten, alcohol, corn, high salt, and high saturated fats. You can identify those that affect you by watching your skin. Oftentimes inflammatory foods make your skin red. You can ask your gut, "Should I eat this?" Oftentimes your gut IQ will lead you to a healthy choice. Chronic inflammation has been linked to psychiatric disorders, diabetes, cardiovascular disease, and cancer. Consider a time when you were doing dishes. Which plates were easiest to clean? The ones with fresh foods or the ones with greasy fats, and cheeses? Consider that you are a vessel just like your dishes. Do you want your insides to be coated and difficult to clean or would you rather consume foods that glide through your body, providing movement, nutrition, and sensuality?

Compassionate Observation Gives Options

The first step is to forgive yourself, have compassion. Then, identify the situations which led to your actions. For example, if you crave french fries every time you have three glasses of wine, you need to either stop at two glasses of wine or stay away from fast food. You woke up feeling greasy and dehydrated and as you washed the slime off your face, you vowed not to do it again. Here is where you can joke with yourself. Oh boy you did it again but at least you didn't hook up with your ex in your moment of weakness or eat a hot fudge sundae and cheeseburger. Dab your puffy eyes and remind yourself how beautiful you are. Once you lighten up, you have room to plan your attack. Maybe join a running group that meets in the mornings. Running on last night's wine and fries just once will make that choice far less enticing. You may even decide that not having wine at all improves your mood and energy level. Your liver will definitely thank you. Whatever you decide, forgiving yourself can lead to a new level of clarity and release guilt. Guilt will never serve you and is frankly an emotion used to control or manipulate you. Release any guilt. It keeps you down and prevents you from moving on to a more loving and accepting state.

Express Your Creativity by Preparing Your Own Food

Get creative; get cooking! Many dishes start with a splash of water in a pan and some chopped onion. Discover which type of onion you like best: sweet Vidalia, green, yellow, or red. Cook the onion until soft on medium to high heat. Then you can add in whichever chopped veggies you like. Know that broccoli, cauliflower, brussels sprouts, and cabbage help remove toxins from your body. Add another splash of water or oil. Consider adding a small amount of grapeseed oil, avocado oil, or fresh pressed extra virgin olive oil. Vegetable oil sounds healthy, but it has been shown to have limited health benefits. Cover to steam the veggies until they are the consistency you like or just stir them in the hot pan until cooked. Season with salt and pepper or a splash of liquid aminos. Serve veggies over a bed of chopped fresh spinach, romaine lettuce, mixed greens, rice, or quinoa.

Start Simply

Note: Himalayan salt, smoked salt, pepper, garlic powder, smoked paprika, parsley, liquid aminos, and herbs de Provence are great seasonings to have on hand. You can make any veggie taste like a culinary delight using one or two of these. Take your time and be patient. Smell your food and delight in your creation. The spices give you important minerals and antioxidants; onions and garlic help with immunity. You are on your way to feeling great.

For quick meals or lunch, consider wraps. You can quickly heat a wrap or tortilla in the microwave (or what I like best is toasting them lightly in the oven or in a skillet) and then spread hummus on it. You can add whatever fresh veggies you have on hand. My favorites are carrot sticks, avocado, green onion, spinach, or mixed power greens and sliced red peppers, and finish with salt and pepper. I find that if I don't have avocado, I like to drizzle my creation with some extra virgin olive oil to make it taste creamier. The base for your wrap can be anything you like: seasoned mashed beans of any kind, hummus, lentils, or even veggie patties.

Pay Attention to Cookware

Inspect your nonstick pots and pans. If you have a coating on your pans, it should be smooth with no irregular colors or chips in it. Make sure it doesn't smell funny when you are cooking. Small flakes of the coating have been known to enter food making people sick. Also take care not to heat pans at a high temperature. It can damage the coating and then it gets into your food. It's great to invest in a quality pan made of stainless steel or ceramic to avoid the nonstick coatings if you can.

Kitchen Pro Tips

If the store only has hard, unripe avocados, I have found that putting them next to a bunch of bananas for two days really ripens them up. Put them in the refrigerator once they are a little soft and they will last for about a week.

Refrigerate fresh mushrooms in paper bag to help them stay fresh and not slimy. Remove them from store packaging when you get home and put them directly in a small paper bag. Fold the bag shut. I use paper lunch bags. Rinse them before using.

To store cilantro, place a bunch in a glass of water and place it on the top shelf of your refrigerator. It looks pretty, reminds you to use it and it will last for weeks.

Quick Breakfast

Do you have a hard time with breakfast? Here's a little something you can make the night before. Smash a large banana in a bowl with a lid. Stir in about ⅛ cup chia seeds. Next add ½ cup rolled oats and 1 ½ cups plant-based milk (You don't need sweetened milk here, watch out for added sugars. The banana makes it sweet.). Combine well, cover, and refrigerate overnight. In the morning, serve with mixed berries, or any fresh fruit you like along with some walnuts or pecans. If you have an extra couple of minutes, toast the nuts. You can eat it cold. So delicious! Cereal is a quick option but take your time and read the nutritional labels paying attention to added sugars. Anything over 7 grams of sugar is more dessert than breakfast.

It's Okay to Skip Breakfast

If you really struggle with breakfast, there may be something your body is trying to tell you. Just skip it! Yes, you can. More and more research is available which suggests many health benefits from intermittent fasting. These include weight loss, increased cell renewal, disease fighting, mental clarity, growth hormone production, and energy. The premise is that when your body is constantly using all its energy to digest, it has little time to repair. Fasting, as long as your doctor says it's okay, can be a very positive thing for your health. Boom, you just got to sleep in an extra ten minutes, or you have time for your morning gratitude practice or a ten-minute yoga flow!

Happiness Starts with Hydration

Even if you are fasting, you still need to drink plenty of water. Starting each day with a large glass of water with lemon or lime, you will provide extra vitamin C and a great way to send your liver some love. The goal is to drink at least half your body weight in ounces of water a day. For example, a 120-pound person should drink 60 ounces of water. Filtering tap water not only reduces common contaminants but also improves the taste. Although plastic water bottles are inexpensive and easy, small amounts of plastic can leach into the water. These plastics are toxins and have been linked to endocrine problems and infertility. You can feel great about using a refillable water bottle because it's not just better for you, but it also reduces your carbon footprint by using less plastic.

Consider adding herbal tea to your hydration habits. Drinking herbal tea helps your body flush toxins and can provide antioxidants. In addition, you may want to consider that health is maintained by daily habits and not seven-day cleanses. Not everyone can handle the expense and the body shock caused by many of the commercially available detox programs. I am not saying they don't work; many people really like them. I am suggesting that daily habits may set you up for a gentler and more cost-effective solution. Herbal teas are convenient hot or cold. A bag of tea in your water bottle will cold brew, giving you refreshment throughout your day.

The Smoothie is Your Tonic Treat

Sea vegetables have been shown to remove toxic metals from your system and cleanse your liver. Powdered spirulina can be taken in a capsule or added to a banana, wild blueberry, dark cherry, and almond milk smoothie without disturbing the taste. Once you are ready to take it to the next level, throw in some baby kale or spinach too.

Anything you can do to support the liver, will support your overall health. The liver is your first line of defense against any toxins. Its job is to filter them out before they enter your bloodstream. This is an amazing process that demonstrates your body's miraculous ability to cleanse and renew. Over time your liver can get taxed and congested. Signs of liver congestion can include feeling foggy, run down, and bloated.

Consider that what you place in your body affects how you feel. How do you want to feel? What or who is preventing you from reaching that feeling? Surround yourself with the people and the things that help you. If certain foods make your face red or blotchy, stop eating them. No matter how much you like them. They are preventing you from being your best self. Make informed decisions for yourself. Know that some foods are addicting, and your addictions and social conditioning may be clouding your judgment. You may notice that you feel bloated, less than comfortable, or even brain fog after eating some foods. Take note and honor your body. You will find that your body can open up to a new level of awareness, health, sensuality, and passion when you honor and feed it as an abundant being of love.

Chapter 6

The Power of Movement and Mindset

Exercise is a great way to release stored up blocks, frustration, hurt, anger, and even excess energy. A healthy sweat clears the pores and releases toxins from your blood and lungs. Movement lubricates your muscles and joints and releases endorphins. It can also help release pent up energy, energy that wasn't burned off when you felt anxiety about a decision or if you had indecision about which action to take. Your hesitation to act may have resulted in anxiety or pent-up frustration stored within the body. Motion can change your mood. Repetitive movement can help free you from the emotions circling inside your head and ground you in your body where you can access your power and freedom. Movement creates ease physically and spiritually because it connects you to your core.

Movement Invites Joy

If you are depressed, you are likely to get fat. If you are fat, you are more likely to be depressed. Obesity is a state of chronic inflammation. Inflammation has been linked to many disease states. Getting out and moving has been shown to decrease stress. Think of exercise as a moving meditation and an energy cleanse. Taking time for yourself honors your body and generates more energy. This movement helps realign your energies and work out stress as well. Exercise is a signal to your body that you cherish it and want to take care of it. In addition, sweating is an awesome cleanse. If you want what's best, exercise is not optional. I don't want to hear that you are not athletic. Start slow and ask your body if it needs more. There is no such thing as wasted time when you are moving or stretching. You can add intensity to your workouts as you feel you need it. Exercise is the ultimate tuning into your body. Your body wants to show up for you. Give yourself permission to be uncomfortable. Give yourself compassion when you just want to move slow and easy. This connection is essential for you to feel through your body. Your energy in the bedroom will also show an increase because you become more connected to the way your body moves and how your heart beats. You can't lose!

You've Got to MOVE IT Devotion

Dear Divine Source, Divinity, God, Goddess, Jesus, Soul Guides, or Loving Angels,

Please help me release my stored-up energy in healthy, productive ways. Guide me to the people and activities which best support me in the highest good and bring me freedom from stagnation. My body benefits from exercise and it aids me in choosing healthy foods to support my desires.

I am joy. Joy I am.

Thank you. Thank you. Thank you.

Message from the Angels: There is Power in Movement

Run—breathless, heart pounding, chest heaving, and eyes steady on the horizon. There are no voices, just your pounding heart and your legs filling with force. Drive and push your feet over the earth and absorb her loving support, her steady presence as a platform for your glorious elation. Your lungs sting and expand pulling in the stream of life, presenting to every cell your mission. You are alive.

And so, it is.

If you don't have the time or the energy for a full workout, yet you feel sluggish or stuck, the following boosts energy and is also releasing.

Shake Out Exercise

Time: 5-10 minutes. Repeat as you feel necessary.

Lie face up on a soft mat or carpet and make sure the area is clear around you. Breathe in deeply. As you breathe out, focus on your fingers and toes. Wiggle and shake them, building intensity to a level you are comfortable with. Next move on to shake and vibrate your arms and legs. Take any pent-up anger, resentment, or hurt and shake it out of your limbs, giving it back to the universe. If you feel any sounds inside you that need to come out, now is the time you can express them. You can do this for as long as you need. It may be pretty intense, but what a rush when you stop and breathe into all the space you created by moving that garbage out! Lie quietly feeling the support of the solid ground beneath you, taking deep, flowing breaths with your eyes closed until you feel completely supported and still.

Mindset Tip

You don't have to work out. You get to work out! Think of it as your play time. How many times have you exercised and thought later, "Boy that was a waste of time!" Never! It's always a great thing to do. Take it slow and tell yourself, "Good job!" You are showing up for yourself. Your mind can clear and reset after moving your body which provides clarity and health. Even if you don't consider yourself athletic, you can be fit.

Ask your body how it wants to move. This is up to you. Oftentimes if you feel stressed and confined, an intense workout is what you need. Think kickboxing, sprints, weightlifting, swimming, or biking. If you are feeling sluggish, you may need a deep stretch, qigong, or a core workout. A brisk walk or a casual swim may be what you need. There are thousands of free workouts online available to you with a quick search. Many community centers offer group classes with little or no cost. There are walking, running, and hiking clubs. Oftentimes a local running store or outdoor store will have access to clubs or groups. Just find what works for you and do it. Carve out the time even if it's just fifteen minutes a day. On weekends you may plan activities that involve being physical as a way to try new things. The benefits will surprise you.

Enjoy Movement in Your Body

Gratitude is more than thanking your body. It's appreciating what it does for you. As you take time to exercise, observe the changes in your body. Compliment yourself. Exercise wakes up your nerves and stimulates blood flow. Movement is your body's expression of joy.

Movement Frees
Your Soul

Circle the things you may try

biking

hiking   gardening

stretching   rock climbing

swimming   jogging

bird watching   yoga

walking during a meeting

dancing: rumba, tango, flamenco

playing sports with your kids

playing fetch with a dog

stand-up paddle boarding

exploring a park

geocaching   tai chi

photography   martial arts

flying a kite

You may imagine yourself as an Olympic hopeful or a wispy butterfly. When lifting weights, you can be superhuman. Be a yoga master in India. Let your imagination take you on a fantasy. Go out and buy those tights or rock comfy sweats. Most importantly, own it. Be comfortable and feel sexy in your workout clothes. Admire your form and glistening body. You can be a superhero when you let yourself.

Give yourself permission to feel your workout as a form of play and expression. You are sexy and powerful.

Sports are a great way to get moving. You will do your best when your body is toned, limber, and strong. Competing can help you focus on your workouts and strive to do better. Just try not to get caught up in winning or losing so that you forget to enjoy the sport. The best way for me to do this, because I am pretty competitive, is to compliment my opponents. I show them gratitude and respect because I really enjoy being pushed and challenged. When they hit a good shot or excel, it makes me want to do it too. Keeping my outlook in appreciation gives me more energy to compete and makes it more fun. Competition can be a form of celebration of the human spirit, drive, and the beautiful human form.

The Forgotten Lymphatic System

The lymphatic system is your body's first line of detox and it's often overlooked. It's not easily detected on radiographic tests. It exists just under your skin, and it helps clear out blockages and manage toxins. Once it gets overtaxed, or clogged, you may experience inflamed or swollen lymph nodes, but you can do a simple thing to help clear it out. Rebounding is the act of standing, completely naked on a trampoline, and taking deep, calm breaths. It can be a small jogging trampoline, I'm not sure how many outdoor trampolines would be able to afford the needed privacy! You want the subtle layer under your skin to move slightly, so nothing can be touching or impeding the skin. Just stand on the trampoline. The springs are causing the perfect vibration and subtle movement to help stimulate your lymphatic system. You can usually sense it first in the back of your throat as things start releasing. Just a couple minutes or twenty deep breaths will accomplish wonders. I take this time to thank my body for everything it has done for me as I prepare for my day.

Chapter 7

Surrender to Your Connections

You are surrounded by voltage or energy: through your thoughts, feelings, words, motion, scents, frequencies, radio waves, microwaves, 4G, 5G, and so much more. There is constant stimulation. You can feel the voltage in flow and harmony, or you can feel it in resistance. Resistance is evident when you ignore. When you pretend that person didn't make your skin crawl, when you rush and forget to feel the sunlight on your face, or when you brush past the person who was trying to smile your way, you have added to the power of resistance. Resistance creates barriers in you, and this can lead to tension. Ignored tension can lead to blockages—the stagnant places in your body where disease can develop, or congestion in areas where your cells can't get what they need. To accept the energy-improving voltage and let the more draining energies flow by or through you, you need to have time and space in which you are quiet and calm. Quiet gives your body a chance to center, balance, and harmonize. It gives you an opportunity to reflect, purge, and choose.

Just Be Exercise

Go to a place where you can be alone. When I first started this practice, I made a sign, "Do Not Disturb" and hung it outside my bedroom door. People still barged in, but it only took some gentle reminders, and a few dirty looks, to convey that my quiet time was not optional. Your environment will test you. That's how you know you are onto something. Get comfy. I have a favorite blanket and sometimes I turn on my salt lamp, diffuse essential oil, or just dab a few drops on my chest. This is your time so pick things you like. Set a timer for five minutes and simply breathe in and out. Relax your eyes and face. Let your tongue lie soft in your mouth. Once your breath is slow and regular and you have told your body that it's okay to just be, you can start to hum. Hum at a tone that feels soft and easy. Let all the air out of your lungs gently and take another breath. Repeat as many times as you like. You are in harmony. Feel your cells connect.

What did you feel or think when you were quiet?

Can you notice the subtle things around you? There are symptoms that you are not living in love. Some call it the ego. It can come from your body trying to protect you or from fear. Chaos and uncertainty can make you feel small and closed up. There are signs that you are operating in ego.

- You feel small and incomplete.

- You feel insignificant.

- You feel scared.

- You aren't listening.

- Things are moving too fast.

- Your heart is racing.

- You find yourself comparing yourself to others.

- You feel jealous.

- You are competing.

- You are judging.

- You feel alone.

- You drink to feel better.

- You shop to feel better.

- You hoard material things for security.

- You find yourself pleasing others or looking for validation.

- You need recognition.

There is nothing wrong with feeling these things. They are normal human emotions and coping mechanisms but if you stay in ego emotions and in a survival mode, you are losing your connections to your divinity and your joy. Joy is fleeting in ego. The ego will be momentarily pleased with a good meal or a new sweater, but the feeling fades. Your love vibration and harmony are silenced when the ego is operating. The secret to feeling joy is in the connections all around you. Please know your ego will never be satisfied because its job is to constantly think about how things could go wrong, how they went wrong in the past, and the illusion of lack.

My Ego is Not Me Rant

My ego is the worst politician ever. It promises me safety if I stay small. If I repeat a predictable pattern, then I will be protected. Mr. Ego, this election I am voting for a different candidate. I am voting for my heart. My heart has much more fun. My heart leads me to giggles and joy. You, Mr. Ego, make me so bland, so predictable, and so boring. You are always measuring and comparing. I hate to pick sides as I know you are just trying to do what you do, and you have protected me so well. I do appreciate you. Sure, I will say, "Hi" when we pass on the street or in the halls. We will always be friends. It's just time. I am independent, unique, and strong. I am ready to live. I know you will continue your campaign and keep sending me emails and pamphlets, but those will just be welcomed reminders of the time when you used to represent me. Now I am representing myself with my heart and my sovereign soul.

Action Step: Stepping Away From Ego. You can do it!

Movement is key here. Ask your child-self how it would like to move. Does it want to dance? Does it want to play an instrument? Go for a walk or run? Maybe your child-self needs to help someone else or have a playdate? Sometimes movement takes place in your mind. It's a decision. A shift in your thoughts from a place of other and separation, to a place of being connected. Take your feelings, and your mind, and tell them that there are other options. Perhaps you show caring to others and genuine interest in those around you. Imagine yourself in the state that is the opposite of ego. You are not judging yourself or participating in negative or suspicious self-talk. You are being compassionate to yourself and recognizing all the goodness around you. There is so much abundance.

Consciousness Devotion

Dear Divine Source, Divinity, God, Goddess, Jesus, Soul Guides, or Loving Angels,

I intend. My intention is to be open to movements inside and around me. I am free to feel these currents and vibrations. I am alive. From this day, I ask to feel it all. This gift of living and feeling gives me power to manifest my life in joy. I wish to let my feelings guide me to my truth. My heart wants to feel. I honor the feelings without comment or judgment. Help me feel safe to connect to everything inside me and around me. I can create abundance in all.

I am light. Light I am.

Thank you. Thank you. Thank you.

Awareness Brings a Feeling of Connection

You are never alone. I am here with you. These words and my intentions are guiding you to a personal paradise. Your ultimate reward is getting to know who you are and how you want to be in this world. You will build trust in the flow because you start to feel and open your heart to the connections around you. This flow makes life unfold more easily. You will still have challenges but in the conflicts, you will have more access to the solutions in flow. You can also return to peace and balance more quickly after a disruption when you practice living in a state of awareness and connectedness.

Listen to Your Wounded, Negative Self

Facing your fears or tender spots and giving them your attention lets them flow out of you and back into the completeness of the Universe. You make room for them by acknowledging them. It's so much better than trying to squash them down or push them away. When you surrender to the pain of hard feelings, they don't control you. They are not yours to keep, only fleeting lessons to learn and release. Holding onto hurt or fear doesn't protect anyone, and it prevents you from showing up for others. Without your unique frequency, the world isn't complete. You are here for a reason. That's exciting. What can you do? What will you do?

Surrendering connections can also be physical. Although symptoms can be anywhere, you want to pay very close attention to pain or tension in your stomach and your reproductive area. If these areas have tension or pain, it is not something to ignore. Any congestion in these areas will prevent you from energizing your life to get what you want done and from experiencing true pleasure. Any pain or chronic tension in your body are signs that you need to be examined by a doctor. Please don't disregard your body. When you seek medical advice, keep asking questions until you feel heard, and the answers make sense. You are the expert of your body. The doctors are there to assist you in healing. Although medications can alleviate symptoms, in my opinion healing does not involve simply prescribing a medicine without looking at the cause. In any case, it's good to have a clear picture of what you expect from your doctors. Many people are happy popping a pill and moving on, but if you want to know how to heal, you need to be clear about your goals. If you do not have a medical condition, this activity can release tension from these areas.

Body Scan Activity

Repeat this daily or more under times of stress.

Dear Divinity, help me to recognize pain and congestion as signs as I honor my body by relaxing it.

Lie down or sit in a comfortable position. Take a deep breath in through your mouth and let it out through your nose. Repeat it ten times. You may need to grab a tissue and you may be a bit dizzy depending on the intensity of your exhale. That's normal.

Return to your normal breathing. Start at the top of your head, place your fingers on the center of your scalp and gently move your fingertips in a massaging motion around your head; notice any tender spots. Stop and go over those areas again; this time send love and care to those spots. You can pretend you are scratching your favorite pet and giving them love and attention. Give that kind of care to yourself. Next, place your hands on your face and feel your fingertips on your eyebrows, cheeks, and chin. Move your shoulders up and down, then forward and back. Lift each leg up and place it gently down. Now, visualize or feel a golden waterfall, gently rinsing down your body from head to toe. The golden waterfall is glistening and warm, soothing your body. Let it rinse away any tension. Welcome to the easy flow. Stay here as long as you feel necessary.

Tension isn't Bad, It's a Signal

Tension can be used as a valuable tool. It's a physical indication of areas in your body which need more self-care. Tension is your body's way of getting your attention. If your shoulders hurt, do you need to stop taking on others' problems? If your stomach hurts, are you holding back from doing your best because of fears of failure or disappointment. It's best to explore any tension or pain because your body is always trying to tell you things. For example, sometimes when I have to say goodbye to someone, my stomach hurts. I used to ignore it and push it down. Now, I say something like, "I'm really going to miss you and I can't wait to see you again." I have honored my body and I let the other person know how much they mean to me. Pretty cool!

Action Step: Exercise in Connectedness

Go outside and simply be. Have no agenda or deadline. Just observe. You can walk or you can simply sit still. Look at the sky and notice any clouds or patterns. Did the angels paint any pictures for you up there? Use all your senses. Do you feel the humidity? Is the sun bathing you? Are the birds singing? Can you locate the bird that sings your favorite notes? Being calm and observant can connect you to the life around you. Take in the nature Mother Gaia has placed around you. Everything has a light and is there to support you. Nature can show you love. You may encounter people during this time. This is a great time to nod, smile, and wave with no expectations, just sharing this special moment of being outside is connecting. If you can take five minutes every day to simply be outside and use all your senses with the intention of being immersed and bringing in light, you will feel Gaia's love and support; your connections and gratitude help all living things as well.

Chapter 8

The New Paradigm

I'm so very tired of the old paradigm of the responsible, productive parts of society not having fun and the underground, hidden, places getting all the sensuality. Why can't you be a loving wife, a mother, and be in touch with primal instincts of lust and sensuality? The tribal society view expects women to be either lusty and behave like a lady of the night or be pure and motherly.

We Don't Need the Labels

We have all heard it. Phrases like: "That's just not ladylike!" or "Good girls don't do that." are used by caring families as a way of protecting little girls as they grow and develop. The reasoning is that these phrases will stop them from going down a path of teenage pregnancy, being negatively labeled, or becoming a victim of sexual assault. But women are just as sexual as men and their sexuality does not cause violent crimes! The good-girl mentality is hurting our families and relationships. It also robs women of a powerful identity that enables them to be confident in saying what they want and what they don't want. Lines get crossed and people are misunderstood when things aren't clear. It's a strong example of how duality is hurting our society.

Every person has both masculine and feminine qualities. We dance between submission and dominance and can draw strength from both. Although the competitive, loud person seems to get all the attention, a soft spoken, wise phrase can move a person to action. A glance can shake the earth. Society has placed expectations upon us, encouraging females to express more submissive and receptive qualities and males to project commanding dominance. We no longer need to be caged into these roles and unattainable expectations. People need to be in touch with both sides. The stereotypical roles are tired and outdated. Men admire and find strong women extremely sexy, and women like to be cherished and nurtured in lovemaking.

In order to come into our wholeness, we need to be free to express both the feminine and masculine aspects of ourselves as we feel and use our imagination and sensuality as guides. You don't have to choose sides. You only need to follow your instincts and know that every choice is perfect at the moment. Even the choices you wouldn't make again were there to ·help you learn and grow. There are no mistakes. Let go of your guilt and shame. They are useless emotions used to control you. If you are not proud of your actions, forgive yourself, ask for forgiveness, and take action to make things right. Center your heart on your desires and move on. Energy is wasted on regret, shame, and guilt. We have so much more to give.

Calling in Love Devotion

Dear Divine Source, Divinity, God, Goddess, Jesus, Soul Guides, or Loving Angels,

Please clear away old beliefs which no longer serve me. Bring me into a new awareness of my body and spirit so that I may feel mystery and joy and be awakened to my unique love frequency. May my spirit attract desire and fulfillment in my relationships and help to bring more love into the world. May I extend grace and forgiveness to myself and unconditional acceptance of my needs. I deeply desire to live in love and grace. Bring me the people to support this love and grace and the environment that supports health and wellness of all types.

And so, it is.

Amen.

Breaking news: There are no good girls. We are all bad girls at times. We are all protective of the things we love. We all have dark places that need to be explored. We can manipulate. We can domineer and we can love with reckless abandon. We need to feel protected and cherished but not demeaned. That's right, no woman is completely bad nor is she completely good. We all have deep, caring hearts and we can express that in different ways. There is nothing wrong with showing every part of your being with the one you love if you choose to. If they can't handle it, it's really not your problem. Usually, the fear that you will disappoint someone is stronger than any possible disappointment. Perhaps you will help them get to the hidden places in themselves. As long as you come from a place of love and respect, you are on the right path. Why go there? Because when you explore every part of your desires and every emotion, you get a gift. The gift is discovering and expressing all parts of yourself. Accepting these gifts gives you power over them. They are unique to you, for you to discover. How you love, what you love, and how you preserve love in your life is up to you.

I Am Perfection and Sacred Feminine Devotion

Dear Divine Source, Divinity, God, Goddess, Jesus, Soul Guides, or Loving Angels,

Help me draw on my sensuality. I am extremely sensitive, powerful, and caring. Help me cherish all parts of my being. I am nurturing and commanding. I can follow and trust my instincts in all situations. At times I may choose to be silent and observe. I am perfection in form. I am sensual because I am alive, my heart is beating so it is. Each beat proves my love, my presence, and my wholeness. I am here to experience and love from the depths of my soul. This love is here for me to cherish myself and reflect my love in others.

I am.

All You Feel is Needed

There are no useless emotions or needs. We need all the energies attached to this human existence. Who is to say one expression of love is better than another? In fact, when you explore basic urges, your primal instincts, you are more connected to the earth. You get the lower vibrations of our earth; those vibrations will ground you, support you and serve as a launching pad to rocket you when you open up to the higher vibrations. We are incomplete without the entire spectrum of emotions and energies. There is no KEEP OUT sign on your loving soul. All the energies are there for a reason. They are part of our purpose for being here on planet earth. If we can share them while taking care of each other, we will come closer to getting our needs met and living the sensual, full, magical, and fun lives we deserve. Consider how happy you can be living a life that truly brings you joy instead of what dogma or society dictates for us. It's through freedom of expression and personal exploration with respect and honor for others, in which we fully express our joy.

Traditional Roles Give Unrealistic Expectations

I would like to propose a revolution. A revolution that is fun, flirty, sexy, and joyful. I hate that people are not free to be lusty with their spouses for fear that they will break a paradigm. I am starting to blame it on those white wedding gowns. Who are we kidding? Wives feel slighted because they want more romance and lust, but they aren't sure how to express it without seeming like a hussy. Partners feel they need to find places to get their needs met because their spouses are cold or seem uninterested. It's a slippery slope and it all comes back to the simple fact that none of us are mind readers, and we are trapped in outdated roles and expectations left over from the old survival and control modes.

Becoming parents adds a whole new dimension to any loving relationship. Let's face it, kids are demanding, and they can be all-consuming. Mix in sleepless nights and some isolation along with hormonal changes and it's a miracle any relationship survives! Suddenly all the tenderness and caring are taken from your partner and redirected to your sweet child. Voids can develop especially when communication breaks down. Dynamics change in a relationship but when you are going through it, it's hard to see it. I'll be honest, sex was not high on my list when my kids were young. What I craved was sleep and an emotional connection. I can only imagine how delighted I would have been had I gotten more foot rubs or nice baths with some chocolates and conversation. I didn't realize how much I needed to be cared for and I certainly was not good at asking. I was not only out of touch with my needs, but I felt guilty for not being overly excited about my partner's needs. Self-deprivation coupled with guilt is not sexy! The only way to be there for your partner is to be honest about your needs and practice self-care. Children provide a non-stop opportunity for self-discovery!

A Life of Love is Constantly Changing

What if you broke free from your beliefs about yourself and your sexual needs? What if you truly accepted all your needs exactly as they are, without judgment? What if your relationships were based on mutual admiration, adoration, respect, and unconditional love? The unconditional love is tricky here. Loving someone no matter what takes away a tired and inefficient model, that old "I will love you if...." paradigm. I will love you if you buy me a big diamond. I will love you if you always agree with me. I will love you if you only want to spend time with me. These conditions are entrapments and recipes for disaster.

What if you just loved because it made your heart sing in that moment? Living each moment for the amazingness that it is involves savoring each sparkle in the eye, each flutter in your stomach, or each heart-pounding caress. We never know when things are going to change, like accidents, illness, or the natural progression of a relationship. Things happen fast and life is unpredictable. Living in love involves deeply loving every moment you can without condition. I believe when your love is returned in this unconditional way, it is at a higher vibration than a love that is based on the I-will-love-you-if conditions. I'm not saying you should throw yourself into physical situations. I am saying that if you feel this person is coming at you with a true heart and you are drawn to them, appreciate your attraction and approach your relationship with the spirit of unconditional love. Do you want to be locked into a love that is based on conditions where you control, or you are feeling controlled? I think that both sides get tired of that dynamic. It's boring and predictable until it falls apart. It falls apart because it lacks the flow and energy of a dynamic love that endures and grows with passion, curiosity, and joy.

Message from the Angels Regarding the Divine Feminine

Dear Beloved One,

Your heart is pure. You say it is not? Believe. Have no doubt because it is so. Let go of the past and regrets. Have confidence in your completeness and loveliness in this moment at this time. You are beautiful and joyful beyond measure. Let your pure light shine and your deepest needs surface. Be solid in your quest for freedom and expression of your heart. Having come from your heart, you have complete grace. Let your happiness show and do not hide from glee. When you are troubled, don't take cover behind a façade. Let your concern ring the bells of awareness. Your loveliness will save this earth from much trouble. Your confidence in knowing what is good and just is needed. We give you strength and grace as the divine feminine cares for everything.

Live in grace dear one.

Chapter 9

Vessel of Love

You want to know how to attract more love and sensuality? Own love. Start with appreciating little things about your body. It's a wonderful thing. Consider the blood pumping through your veins and arteries. It carries healing oxygen, nutrients, and protection to areas in need and takes away toxins. Your body has a grid of electronic impulses firing through your tissues creating pulses of life around you. You can channel the energy of your blood and the charge of your nerves to give and receive. It all starts with the breath and your intention.

Your body is a gift to cherish and nurture. Make friends with it. Each morning, tell it you appreciate everything it does for you. Honor what your body has done and will do for you. Ask your body how it feels. Breathe in and really be present with every cell, muscle, and thought. This body scan can tell you many things. If your mouth is dry, make sure you have a nice glass of water before your coffee or tea. If your muscles are tight, you may want to stretch more deeply after your workouts. You may have a different opinion about last night's dinner, when you wake up the next morning and note how you feel.

The point is to really notice yourself waking up and be present with the gift of your body. You will find that making great food and sleep choices will be easier once you feel the positive impact it can have upon your body. Your body will respond with more energy, clear thinking, and passion from within. Every morning before you rise, give praise. It goes like this:

Morning Exercise

Dear body, thank you for giving me another day.

Take a deep breath.

Thank you, my precious heart, for pumping my blood, helping me to keep my brain in check, and helping me live in joy.

Take a deep breath.

Thank you muscles for holding my bones.

Take a deep breath and stretch each leg long and your arms over your head.

Thank you eyes for seeing this world.

Take a deep breath.

Thank you wonderful mouth for the breath, tastes, and speech you provide. My lips are so soft and sensitive.

Take a deep breath.

Thank you, my awesome lungs, for bringing in cleansing and energizing oxygen for my mind and blood.

Take a deep breath.

Thank you, incredible organs for working in synchronicity without asking anything from me.

Set your intention and request that the loving presence of God, Goddess, Spirit, or Angels accompany you throughout your day. They are beings of light who wish to help you and make your day easier. All you have to do is ask by inviting them in. We are energetic beings. Our bodies want to take in energy. Imagine love and light from the angels of God showering down and bringing peace and healing from your head all the way down to your toes. Pick the shade of color you identify with and feel the healing and rejuvenation that it provides as it floods through your body. Thank the thousand angels who support you for their help and invite them to be with you during your day.

Daily Intention Devotion

Angels, I invite you into my day, today and every day, to show me the highest good and help me bring joy and light to the world as I bring forth the highest expression of this day.

Thank you. Thank you. Thank you.

Cherish Your Body

As you enter your day, give gratitude to your body. Give yourself at least four compliments. It can be anything at all. Here's some to get you going: I am so grateful for my strong legs. My eyes are pretty and bright. I have the softest arms. I am amazed at how lovely my body moves. I love my voice. People are so lucky to have me in their lives. You may find it easier to compliment yourself when you are taking your morning shower. I know this may be a classic, fake it till you make it situation in which you are forcing yourself to produce compliments and you may not even agree completely with everything you say. It's okay because your brain and your body are still receiving compliments and that's what matters. So, as you lather each body part, mentally complement each part of you. You are cherishing yourself. Your body will respond.

Self-Knowledge, Give Yourself Freedom to Feel

Know your body. What do you like? Explore different touches, pressures, and rhythms. If you have been ashamed or told that touching yourself is something unbecoming, this is a paradigm that needs to crash down right now. You have this wonderful body filled with a complex nervous system designed to take in subtle changes in pressure, temperature, and even intention. Yes, your body knows intention. If you touch yourself with the intention of pleasing yourself, it's going to work out really well. In the same vein, if you touch your lover with the intention of blowing their mind or taking them to another place, you are setting yourself up for a real connection. Knowing and honoring what you like can elevate your experiences. The joy in being present with yourself and for yourself is empowering and extremely sexy.

Message from the Angels About Your Unique Needs

Dear One,

Turn, turn, and turn, you feel the burn and the yearn. Pushing it down it saturates in sadness. A quiet place in your soul can tell you the release: the fulfillment and your joy. You are a divine soul with unique abilities to love in your special way. The world needs your love vibration. The earth craves your happiness. When you are satisfied, she sighs with pleasure.

And so, it is.

Your Unique Love Vibration is Perfect in this Moment

Feel and cherish what is uniquely you. Embrace and stroke the oneness in you. People may have tried to protect you from being your unique self. It was not safe, and you trusted those trying to protect you. It's a new day. The walls of protection are not needed. Your unique self doesn't need to hide. You have the choice to live in the love vibration and recognize when the sneaky fear emotions try to take hold. Do not be angry with your fear. Greet it; know that it's a natural response but choose how you want to redirect it. Open the sanctuary and feel the pulse of your heart. The clarity in your veins is yours. Whatever you feel, dark or light, is in pure perfection. The things that give you a spark are clues to your contribution and unique talents. Honor your spark. The old beliefs fall away. Having confidence and security in your divinity frees you to see the divinity in others. This connection is both primal and angelic. Remember the first step is being one in yourself first.

My Heart Knows ALL Devotion

Dear Divine Source, Divinity, God, Goddess, Jesus, Soul Guides, or Loving Angels,

I know I am a loving being. Help my heart open up to the loving energy around me. As I place my right hand over my heart, I feel the pulse of my life force. I am here for a reason and that reason centers around love. Help me to surrender to my purpose. I will know my purpose when I experience true joy. Help me listen to the questions and doubts within me that tell me I am not good enough or unworthy.

I need to feel those doubts and recognize how they affect me. We all have doubts; don't push them away, don't ignore them, honor them, thank them, and release them. Acknowledging my doubts and honoring them helps me connect to my soul purpose. Once they are released, I have space to soar.

And so, it is.

Be Curious About What Lights You Up

As you make space to see perfection around you and gain clarity with what you want, you will be more open to arousal. Men can show it easily. Women on the other hand, although wanting to be close and connected, are more like a combination lock than a flagpole. Sometimes the combination to our lock needs to be spun around a few times! We feel our way to complete arousal and each time can be completely different. Your body is alive with needs and rhythms. It may be your heart thumping in your chest, or a tightness in your core accompanied by a nervousness or even an intensity. Get quiet and feel what your body is telling you. What do you like? What turns you on? There are no wrong answers. It's so much fun!

The magic is in the idea that when you show up as yourself and in your most centered, confident, self-assured way, you are taking care of your own needs. Love will emanate from your pores. That kind of love is enticing and irresistible to everyone! It's the feeling that no matter what you have, you and your happiness are complete—not dependent on whether or not someone else shows up for you. Your complete self-love and gratitude spiral together creating an abundance of joy. This abundance shows others what is possible. Confident self-love helps others access their joy.

Perfect Passion Devotion

Dear Divine Source, Divinity, God, Goddess, Jesus, Soul Guides, or Loving Angels,

Because I breathe, because my heart beats, I need pleasure. I invite my pleasure to me; I breathe it into my heart and my heart responds. My body is open and willing to receive. I am blessed in being gifted this pleasure center of my body. I invite the energy to flow through me and let my body open up to the energies. Let them envelope me, move me, absorb deeply within me. Passion isn't from the outside; it comes from deep inside my soul. Let me feel free to release my passion in its many forms. I am open to it overcoming me. Let my spirit sing, moan, and scream. Every part of me is perfect and designed to bring me pleasure.

And so, it is.

Be Present

Thoughts and fears are what your brain attaches to experiences. Your brain places layers on your experiences in an attempt to protect you. The only escape from your brain dulling your senses or adding fear-based emotions that can dilute your happiness is complete immersion in the present moment. Diving into the present and experiencing it with all your senses lets you have an experience without fear. True freedom and sensuality come from being in a primal state without thoughts. You simply need and you open yourself up to completing another's needs. Giving them your complete presence is the ultimate gift. Being free from fears is a complete state of bliss.

FEAR-BASED

ACTIONS AND EMOTIONS

Fatigue
Anxiety
Worry
Panic
Being Boastful
Negativity
Not Asking for Help
Avoidance
Feeling Lonely
People Pleasing
Dishonesty
Feeling Worthless
Comparing
Competing

Action Step: Fear vs. Love

When you recognize the fear-based states showing up, notice how you feel physically. You may notice patterns of when fear-based states show up or reoccurring physical pain. You can't stop these symptoms, but you can spend less time there once you have control over them by simply being aware of them. Chose an emotion or state from the Love-Based Emotion Chart to help shift your focus to a state that is more supportive to joy and happiness. Sometimes it takes time, but if you keep your intention on where you want to be and keep asking for help, it will happen for you. These are small adjustments that make big changes over time. Happiness is your birthright but only you can claim what it means to you.

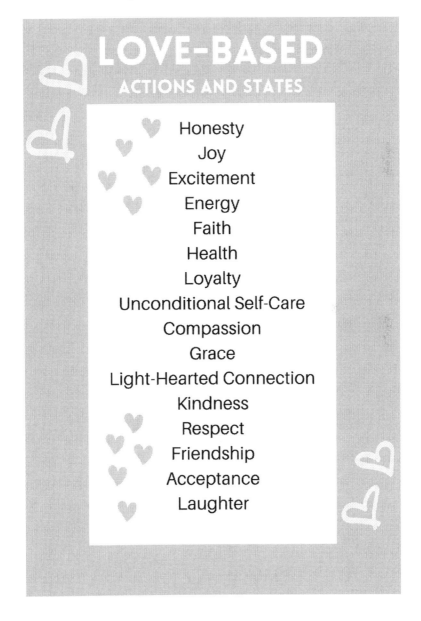

LOVE-BASED
ACTIONS AND STATES

Honesty
Joy
Excitement
Energy
Faith
Health
Loyalty
Unconditional Self-Care
Compassion
Grace
Light-Hearted Connection
Kindness
Respect
Friendship
Acceptance
Laughter

My Lover Devotion

Dear Angels of Love,

I ask you to please surround my lover with care. Let them feel their divine connection to good, tenderness, and strength. May they feel and sense my loving connection to them. I release my expectations knowing that you will provide the highest expression of our connection, whether in the physical or spiritual realms. The angels know our limitless ability to love; please show us in a gentle way how we can love each other for the highest good of humanity. We shake with joy in your light!

Thank you. Thank you. Thank you.

PART THREE

Dynamic Love

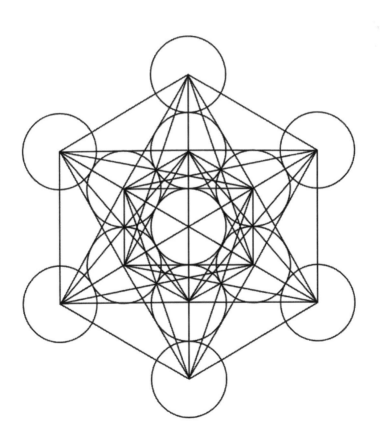

Chapter 10

Expectations

Being completely clear on what you desire from your partner is much easier than explaining what you don't want. Approaching your relationship from a feeling of peace and a clear vision provides a calm retreat in which you can both feel safe. The other option is to react to your partner and tell them what you don't want from a feeling of frustration. I've had trouble with this, and I will be the first to admit it. Here's the problem: Life gets messy. You get pulled in many directions and then there are emotions and hormones thrown in. Yes, I react differently depending on the moon and my cycle. I have tracked it. It's real. My feelings, however, are also real and I must honor them no matter what time of the month it is or where the constellations are positioned in the sky. It's just that the environment can, let's say... enhance my feelings. So, if I can be clear as to what's important to me, oftentimes I can navigate my strong emotions and get back to a stable mood. Then I can let the less important stuff fall away. Being completely clear on what you want empowers you to take responsibility for your wants and needs. Here's how you do it.

Know Your Why

This is all about you: How you want your relationship to look and feel will drive your why. What is really important to you? Only you can answer it. This may change and categories may overlap. Once you have your top three, you can start to decide which things you want to focus on improving and the things you will let go. When you love from a focused why, you can be centered on a life of love. There are no wrong answers. Here are some foundations you could pick from or think of your own. Think along the lines of what brings you the most joy and the most joy to your partner. Also take this time to honor what is positive in your relationship. What's going great? What are your common triggers?

Pillars of Relationships

Trust: Maybe this looks like open communication and a pact to share, really share, and not hide things from each other.

Teamwork: Focusing on working together to make things happen. This could be raising children, caring for pets, projects, charities, or volunteering together.

Financial Security: Making money may be more important than spending lots of time together and financial security can be comforting to a relationship.

Quality Time Together: Maybe the quality of life is better when you can spend more time together. It may look like working from home or having a job with flexible hours. Maybe it's cherished weekends because you are so busy during the week. Spend fun time together.

Friendship: How do you treat your friends? Is it important for you to feel a kinship with your lover? What do you expect from your friends? If you have fallen out of friendship with your lover, how can you recover? A shared interest can really build your friendship.

Physical Connection: Consider the amount of sex you need and your definition of intimacy: the connection of lovemaking may be different depending on the ebb and flow of life, but do you need it to feel connected and how much? Do your expectations match theirs? Also consider how other physical connections such as hand holding, playing footsie, snuggling on the couch, foot massages, brushing your hair, showering together, etc., can be bonding to your relationship.

Division of Household Duties: Are there things you absolutely don't like doing in the house? Can the cooking or shopping be divided? What things are you okay with and which would you rather delegate?

Physical Attraction: Do you need to see muscles on your lover to be turned on? Is a spare tire sexy or do you need a six pack? It's okay to be honest about what turns you on, but when you really get serious about your top three, maybe this one has some flexibility. Nobody is getting younger. Maybe you focus on what is most physically attractive about your partner? Would you like them to reveal how you excite them?

Communication: No matter how much you love someone, it's impossible to read their minds and unfair to assume. Many relationships thrive with open communication. Trust is built and maintained by communication. Communicating what you are happy about and the future can fortify your bond.

- Compliments and Admiration: How often do you need to hear that you are appreciated and honored? Special compliments can be very meaningful.

- Bringing up Areas of Concern: Is there a neutral way to address concerns? How does your partner want you tell them when you feel let down? Is there a better time of the day to discuss things that need resolution? Some people need to get it out right away and some would like to decompress before trying to solve problems.

- Stimulating Conversation: Maybe you need to have dynamic conversations. You could talk about movies, books, or politics and that helps you feel connected to your partner.

- Tone and Volume: What tone of voice is your favorite? What brings you comfort and security? Is it a clear deep message? Do you like it when they talk softly or with a strong volume?

- Phone Calls or Texts: Do you like to get flirty texts and phone calls during the day or would you rather save up and talk at the end of the day.

- Routines: Is it important to know your partner's schedule so you can think of them at different parts of the day? Think about how you like to feel connected. Many women feel more in touch with their sensuality, trust, and intimacy the more their partners communicate with them. Building strong communication can lead to some hot loving.

- Honesty: How do you communicate in their language? Since the masculine tends to express in the physical, it helps to assure them that the physical is important to you as well. But also suggest ways they can meet your needs for a caring connection. Your mind is telling you to ignore them so they can feel what you feel, or be short with them, but that is a long hard road. You risk building resentment and pushing them further away. If they picked up on your needs, you wouldn't be ignoring them in the first place. Can you see the vicious cycle? Do what your heart says: ask for a hug; tell them you miss time with them; tell them about a favorite memory you have with them; if you feel alone, tell them. Perhaps you say something like, "I'm thinking of the ways I want to be close to you. I'd really like a date night," "Can we take a walk after dinner?" or simply hold their hand.

Open to your Desires to Create Fantasies

Envision your fantasy. What is the ultimate connection you can imagine having with someone else? Do you see it as role-playing back and forth? Maybe you want to be romanced with flowers and chocolates. There are so many scenarios! Maybe you would like to re-live the feeling of a high school dance and hide in the back seat of your car stealing kisses and getting felt up after curfew? There is nothing wrong with fantasies; in fact, your mind and heart can come up with really great things. Personally, I find high school memories and fantasies are pretty powerful. Maybe it's all the hormones or how everyone had cut abs and nice hair back then. But I'd say whatever works, do it! I love nature and I can tell you that pleasing your lover at night next to a tree with the moon looking on is sublime. Maybe it's them discovering you aren't wearing panties. Finding the mystery and playfulness is part of the fun. Be free. You deserve to feel passion and share it. Your body needs to move to show your divinity. And it's fun!

Pleasure Principles

- Surprise: You don't know where or when, but you know you are going to get it!

- Anticipation: You set a time and look forward to it, or your lover teases you with whether or not it's going to happen.

- A candle lit room

- Urgent and forceful

- Slow burn with lots of foreplay

- Soft music

- Loud music

- Shaved clean

- Dirty and sweaty

- Fresh from the shower

- Flirty eye contact

- Hugging and whispering after

- Falling asleep in their arms

- Positions you like, the positions your lover likes

- Eye contact

- Blind fold

- Massage

- Oils and lotions

What's your pleasure? _____

Feedback and communication create a loving dance between your bodies. Your lover wants to see and feel reactions from you. Your response can guide them to giving you deep pleasure. The obvious is grabbing or caressing them. However, consider touching yourself as they are touching you. Make it all about your pleasure until you sense it's time for them. Tell them when it's good. There are no wrong sounds to make. Anything you do is fun and sexy when you are intimate. The more unusual and unique the better! This is about you, and nobody can love the way you do! I'm smiling thinking about it! Look at your beautiful body: the wonderful contours and your soft skin; your body is made to love and be loved. It needs to move and express that love. Ask them what they want you to do to them. Look them in the eyes. You are a sexy, vibrant being of light.

Get Quiet and Tune into You

Giving into your desires takes awareness. Stop and feel what your body needs. It may need to surrender to rest. Stopping and giving yourself what you need involves awareness and trust. Sometimes it means trusting that things will work out and you don't need to be in control. Give in to your feelings and desires and trust that your partner is there to provide. The Universe brought you together and you fulfill something within them which no one else can, and they complete you in a way no one else can. It's a dance of the souls where our bodies become expressions of freedom and trust. You enter a timeless space where all that matters is that touch, receiving it, and surrendering to the feelings, being in the moment with an open heart. We are not guaranteed another day, another minute. How would you love if you had no expectation, only surrender?

Asking for What you Want Devotion

Dear Divine Source, Divinity, God, Goddess, Jesus, Soul Guides, or Loving Angels,

Give me courage to ask for what I want. I realize that depending on others can make me feel vulnerable. But help me see that surrendering to my needs and telling others how they can be there for me, is worth the risks or fears that sometimes hold me back from the joy and connections around me. Help me tune into myself so that I can share my unique qualities and find more love in expressing them. I am aware and present to myself.

And so, it is.

Thank you. Thank you. Thank you.

Even though opposites attract, it's hard work to keep the tension of opposites up for the long term. It's much more efficient to go with the flow and attract what you want by giving what you want to receive. All of the sudden you are the center of their world, not by demanding your needs, but by showing them how to love you. However, if you can talk it out from an area of love and connection, you can illuminate aspects of your love which will bring you closer together. You will learn about how they think and what their feelings are if you can come from your heart space and resist letting your mind tell you all the reasons you are disappointed. Just listening and being open can move you beyond hurt and to more joy.

Routines Can Dilute Passion

We are creatures of habit and habits tend to produce the same result over and over. It's predictable and efficient. When it comes to sex, habits tend to lean away from the erotic. No one would ever brag about being boring in the bedroom. Expressing sensual love and giving loving touch can never come with expectation of the final act of climax as the sole purpose. A routine can lead to a robotic and insincere experience. There is no recipe for passion. There are ingredients that come together in an erotic alchemy. You get this sacred time to spend with another person. Why dilute it with a preconceived notion of what it should be or expectations? Isn't it better to be surprised and pleased? Many times, living in the moment can be much better than what you had planned. Let your lover surprise you. The adventure is in not knowing what feelings and sensations may come to you. It's an exercise in surrendering in the moment, to feelings and touches, and letting them take you on an adventure.

Being Present with Your Desire

You are a divine being of light and your lover is too! Honor this sacred space between you. Your bodies represent your divine souls in action at every moment. Enter your union with the remembrance of your sacred power of giving and receiving love. Giving pleasure involves the intention of pleasing that person. You desire to see them pleased. Think of how that perspective opens your heart to the ultimate experience. Time stands still as you zone in on their body's response to your explorations and curiosity about their pleasure. Breathe into your heart and into your hands as you explore the ways your touch can ignite your lover. Involve all your senses. Simply syncing up your breath helps you tune into your partner's state and desires. Inhale the delight. Really let them see you and submit to being seen. Let your voice express your sensuality. Enter the timeless space of desire.

Your Body is Designed for Pleasure

Your amazing nervous system is a superhighway to pleasure. The vagus nerve is the largest nerve running through your body. It has been associated with non-vaginal orgasms. Believe it or not, people who are paralyzed can experience orgasms. To me it's not a coincidence that the vagus nerve is the primary nerve for your voice and your tongue. Kissing and making pleasure sounds ignite this nerve and your pleasure zones throughout your body. Let your voice express your sensuality. Try different patterns, intensities, and rhythms. Know that the power of touch and intention, along with surrender, are the keys to your loving expression. Let your nervous system deliver a delightful and all-consuming experience! Whew!

Deep Pleasure Devotion

Dear Divine Source, Divinity, God, Goddess, Jesus, Soul Guides, or Loving Angels,

Help me make the decision to open my body to ecstasy in all its forms. My spirit craves freedom to fly, explore, and satisfy. I realize past trauma can block or create places of density in my spirit. I choose to open the channels and accept pleasure. I realize there are many forms of pleasure and I choose to accept and channel forms that support my highest good. Help me see less than optimal patterns in life so I can identify them and choose a higher good. I am a powerful force of divinity, and all my choices are perfect for me at that time. There is no reason to dwell in the past as my light and strength are here in this moment.

Thank you. Thank you. Thank you.

Amen

You are Here to Love

You can expect that your loving touch will bring pleasure. Our bodies were designed to channel energies. We can even change the energy patterns in others just by entering a room. You can expect that the way you are feeling will make a difference to everyone around you. Your waking up this morning was validation that your energy is needed and wanted. It is part of the communal network of energy on the grid of the earth. Your intentions and expectations for goodness and love will be felt. Your loving energy will draw others to you.

Open to Love Devotion

Dear Divine Source, Divinity, God, Goddess, Jesus, Soul Guides, or Loving Angels,

I feel the energy pulsing through my body. Help me to show my true soul to the world. I know that I will attract others with the same love frequencies. Show me how my love vibration is mirrored in my world. Help me to see love in my surroundings. Flowers, trees, birds, and animals are likely to show me love when I am in a state of gratitude and appreciation. Help me use all my senses to connect with the abundance around me. It is there for me when I choose to see it and connect with it.

Thank you. Thank you. Thank you.

The Heart Shares

Your heart opens to experiences around it. The common assumption is that the brain is the most powerful organ, but the heart produces the highest energy emitted from your body. Feeling sensual and sexually energetic requires an open heart and a strong connection to the earth. Prepare to be overcome when you involve your whole heart.

Opening the Heart Exercise

Sit quietly. Calm your mind and try not to think. Thinking is the buzzkill of sensuality and calmness. Breathe deep clam breaths into your heart. Feel it with lightness and wholeness. If you sense places in your heart which are hardened or stiff, focus the next breath on gently releasing the tension. Fill that stuck space with new air and life. Envision a calm pink color around your heart. Next, take that calm, happy heart for a walk outside or at least around your surroundings. Greet each thing quietly with a loving gaze and your heart's appreciation. You can lightly touch objects and plants or just gaze at them. Do what feels best. If conflict with people or situations come up as you focus on your heart, forgive them and recognize that they brought you to the special place you are today. Thank them and release them as you keep breathing in goodness and healing. A golden beam seals the goodness of your heart and bonds you to unconditional love.

Men Have Needs

For the masculine energy there are some things which tend to undermine a relationship if they are not addressed. In general, the masculine needs to feel affirmation, openness, connection, and acceptance not criticism. The masculine is reassured when he is in control. Taking control away typically leaves a man feeling helpless and unhappy in a relationship. Telling him how he should dress, how he should spend his time, or criticizing him would be examples to try to control him. Even if he acts as if it's okay, it will erode the relationship. Men like to be heroes and save the day. Playful acknowledgment of their strengths and smarts helps them see how important they are to you. Men typically show love by doing. Let your man know how he can protect you and why you cherish him. Telling him makes him amazing in the bedroom. Men like to express love physically but the dynamic and the beautiful dance of shared sensuality happen when he can recognize his partner's need for connection, communication, and safety and meet those needs with the same urgency he has for his physical release of love making.

Women Need to Feel

For the feminine energy generally, there are three basic needs as well. Simply, most women need to feel safe. She needs to feel like she is number one in her partner's life and that her needs are understood. She needs to be seen and verbally assured that she is seen. Women who are lonely and feel their partner is distracted or not paying them enough attention will typically close up and make themselves less available physically and mentally. When asked if she is okay, she will typically say, "I'm fine," but the wise partner will know that she is not fine, and that she needs more. In addition to being safe and seen, women need to feel open communication to trust. He needs to communicate that his heart space is with hers. In this situation if you have children, the mother may just direct her love to her children, because they are easier to love. They have no expectations, and they just give back because that's all they know. It's easy to love your kids and pets. It's harder to be intimate if you feel your partner doesn't even notice you. Can you relate?

How can your partner expect you to be aroused and have joy when they are not giving you the attention or communication you need? Let's put it this way: If they aren't noticing your new panties, there's a chance they are depressed, spending time with porn, exhausted, or feel like their needs aren't being met. Regardless, you need to have a sit-down talk. Do not accept being ignored or disregarded. You are sexy and worth attention, and you deserve to get the attention you want.

Men are not trained in this just as women are not trained in this either. After all the endorphins of new love wear away, the only way to let someone know how to love you is to tell them. Tell them when they are doing well and lovingly guide them to nurture your needs. Being honest about your needs and being compassionate with each other can keep your relationship growing and bring you more joy and in turn bring the world more joy.

I am Desire Devotion

Dear Divine Source, Divinity, God, Goddess, Jesus, Soul Guides, and Loving Angels,

Help me to connect to my lover. Raise my awareness of his breath, his heartbeat, and his desire. As I connect to his pulse and breath, I can feel his arousal. It is there for me to play with. I have power to create change and growth. It's never more evident than the visible arousal of my man. May I cherish his attraction to me and see how I am a cause of much love and desire. It is joy and fulfillment. I am sensual and erotic.

Thank you. Thank you. Thank you.

Your body is constantly adapting and receiving. It can also be an amazing vessel for wonderful pleasure and circuitry. It has to do with surrender and being in the present moment. This quiet focus on pleasure allows you to feel with greater intensity. This pleasure is intensified with vocalization and movement. The vocalizations can be sounds or words. This is a personal thing to be determined and experimented by you and your partner. Just have fun with whatever you decide. Also, your intention to share pleasure and love can be felt by your partner. This dance of giving and taking is electric and compounding.

Fantasies Create a Playground

Fantasies are crazy things and so different for everyone and I think that's the best part of them. Each person has their own definition of an ultimate fantasy. Whether your intimate fantasies are centered around muscles, authority, the forbidden, domination, submission, secrets, superheroes, or experiences, they are unique to you and may be always changing. Do you want your partner to wear something sexy, cook a special dinner for you, light some candles, draw a bubble bath, shower you with flowers, tie you up, blindfold you, tease you, spank you, compliment you, smell clean, smell sweaty, be loud, whisper, be authoritative, or be sweet? I can go on and on.

Expressing Fantasy Devotion

Dear Divine Source, Divinity, God, Goddess, Jesus, Soul Guides, or Loving Angels,

Help me connect to my fantasies. I know my partner isn't a mind reader, so it helps to give him ideas and ways to connect to me. Help me express my needs in a loving and open way so that we can pleasure each other and strengthen our bond of love and respect. I realize that some things may seem erotic in my imagination, and they may not play out as I expect. I will have a sense of humor and appreciation in my partner when he listens and explores my needs with me.

Thank you. Thank you. Thank you.

Fantasy Exercise

Write all your wildest fantasies on strips of paper. Then fold them in half and put them in a bowl. Tell your partner you want to have a fun date and that you have prepared some sexy strips for them. This will usually pique some fair amount of interest. Depending on their comfort level, they may indulge you or simply tease you with the new information you have provided for them. If you do this, you will be surrendering intimate information to them. Please know that they may or may not do anything with this information. Watch your expectations. Let them surprise you. You just don't know. Please be open with them and tell them if their response pleases you. If you are not pleased, you have space for a conversation or suggestion. A simple phrase like, "I was thinking…." can open up a dialogue. Most of all, approach this with an open heart and love. You can ask them, "Do you want to play a game?"

Connection Also Takes Surrender

Surrender doesn't mean giving up or not caring. It means setting your intention and trusting that it will work out once you have done what you can do to help it along. Mentally forcing something to happen rarely works out. For example, if you set an intention to focus on reaching a climax and only are concerned about reaching a state of ecstasy, you will rarely reach it. True, intense, and meaningful orgasms take enjoyment and being in the moment, trusting that you are whole and lovable while surrendering to the wave of pleasure. The journey is absolutely part of the reward!

Bedroom talk

It may come naturally to some people. But I can admit, I had to work on it. Start by making sounds, just let them out. Your lover appreciates feedback. If that kiss on your neck lights you up, let out a moan or a sigh. Often your eyes can intensify any experience. Encourage and ask. "What if I did ___ to you? Do you like this? Do you know what I dreamt about? I think about you when _____."

How about the voices in your head? Come on, I know you have an internal dialogue when you are making love. Everybody does it! *Man, maybe I should do more core? Does this new natural deodorant work? Or should we paint this room?* I know random thoughts pop into your head or questions about what your partner is thinking. You may be a distracted lover. Being present takes practice but oh my goodness, if you get good at it, you will be blown away! I'm pretty sure your partner won't mind if you practice on them.

Connect to Divine Goddess Within Devotion

Dear Divine Source, Divinity, God, Goddess, Jesus, Soul Guide, or Loving Angels,

Help me connect to my divine Goddess of sexiness. Give me freedom to release self-consciousness and move my body in union with my divinity. I am a powerful, sexy force of attraction. Help me use my eyes to open up to the soul of my partner and connect every dimension of our union. I love with my entire body and enjoy with rhythmic pulsing. My being is alive with pleasure to share. I know what feels best to me at the moment and I tell my partner my needs.

And so, it is.

Being Attentive Creates More Connection

Life can be repetitive and predictable. How do you mix it up? Eat dinner in a different place. Pay attention to what may be distracting you: your phone, the TV, children's chatter, or pets? Many things try to take our attention. Remember one the most basic and powerful human desires is to be noticed and acknowledged as being important. You want to be cherished? Then you have to be willing to cherish your partner. How do you tune in and really be there for them? Find what is important to them by actually asking them. Listen like you would have on your first date. What makes them feel loved and connected to you? How do you show each other that you have a cherished friendship?

Watching TV Together: Don't Become Zombies

Note: Be careful with watching TV as a means of connecting with your partner. It's easy to tune out and use entertainment as an escape. It's okay to do this, but realize this activity is not necessarily bringing you closer. The important thing to pay attention to is if you are watching together or just using the TV to relax or zone out. I know that if my partner says he wants to watch golf, he really wants to nap on the couch. So, I will call him out on it and either take a nap with him on the couch or take the time to get something done that I want to do alone. You may like the feeling of snuggling under a blanket while watching TV or the feeling of your partner playing with your hair. Did you ever wonder why they call what's on television programming? Pay attention to what you are exposing yourself to. Is it raising your vibration or simply programming you? Are you enjoying this time or is it distracting you from your joy?

Every Couple Needs Quality Time

Ultimately the things that bring you joy, the things that light you up, will be the things you will want to share with your loved ones. It may not even be the activity itself, but the time you have taken to be together that makes it special. Question what you do. Why do you like it? When you finish your special activity with your loved ones, no matter how big or small, connect with them and tell them how special it was to you. How much you appreciated it and what fun it was. Gratitude is contagious. Sharing your appreciation with those around you is magical. When you compliment people around you, you show that you see them, and they are important. Compliments help you connect with others or simply brighten their day. When you seek to see goodness in others, it opens up the goodness in you and melts barriers.

Honesty with Your Needs

Be honest. If you want to make love but feel like there's something in the way, you need to talk about it. Making love with weight on your heart is shallow and formless and can leave you feeling empty. You can have sex and get a release but making love and loving takes not just your body but also your soul investment. If you have questions, concerns, feelings half explored, it's best to clear those before you can enter your loving zone of intimacy. Your lover will want to help you feel centered and comfortable because when you share your total being, the feeling is like nothing else. Your connection is irreplaceable and addictive. It's about sharing and your partner being there for you. Maybe there is something going on with your body or mind on that day. Being honest about how you feel honors your needs. Once you show them yours, they can feel safe showing theirs. Sharing will bring you closer and strengthen your bond. You may fear that they can't handle your complete honesty. Isn't it better to know that than hide from it? There is no one who can bring joy the way you do; sometimes there is some unwrapping of feelings or fears to get to the joy. A life of love takes bravery and honesty. It's okay to start small. Feel free to put your toes in the water before you jump off the edge. Or just count to three and jump in. It's up to YOU!

Abundance Devotion

Dear Divine Source, Divinity, God, Goddess, Jesus, Soul Guides, or Loving Angels,

I am alive for a special purpose and my life has an impact on everything. Help me determine with clarity my path in each decision to recognize fear or lack as illusions. I choose to find joy and abundance and look for ways to add more joy and abundance to those around me. Being open to joy will bring my body more pleasure and I will recognize the loving things my partner does for me when my heart is open. Please help me keep my heart open and share my love energy with those around me. My loving gaze can transform the world around me.

And so, it is.

Thank you. Thank you. Thank you.

Chapter 11

Danger of Duality

Duality is something powerful to recognize. Recognizing it helps change a fixed mindset. Anytime you have a fixed mindset, you are in opposition to the world and your flow in the world because the world does not work in absolutes; it's constantly evolving. Making judgments about yourself and others is a sign you are coming from a place of duality. Since things are always changing and evolving, we need to constantly adapt. Another problem with duality is that it makes someone right and someone wrong. It's definitive and divisive and it destroys grace. Holding onto a belief and picking sides creates a fixed mindset and gives the ego power. Ego and judgment will find ways to take you away from joy and beautiful sensuality. There's no middle ground in duality and no curiosity as to what your opposition's viewpoint might be.

Message from the Angels about Freedom from Judgments

Dear Ones,

We want you to know grace. You are worthy of grace and ease. You can move through your life and your feelings with grace by being present as an observer. We care for you. You are never alone. When you feel hurt or isolated, be present and stay calm. From a place of respect for your feelings, speak your heart and focus. Ask your heart, what is your ultimate truth. How can you honor that truth? Let that truth guide you to grace; grace to be kind, understanding, and forgiving to yourself.

And so, it is.

Judgments Cause Divisions

Think about some of the judgments we make every day. The absolute judgments are tricky and very hard on us. They are hard on our families, our communities, and our country. They polarize our thinking and make us critical, but what good does that do? Often a judgment involves supporting that position so that you defend it when someone else has a different opinion. Duality separates us and makes us simple and controlled. Accept that there is always more than a single answer. It depends on what you know and your past. Every person is entitled to their views as long as they are not hurting someone else.

When there is an attempt to make someone quiet or an obvious attempt to cause division and censorship, I see a power struggle and an attempt to control. We have the human right to decide. Does this make sense to me? What about it makes it beneficial? Does this idea still work for me and those around me? Just because something has been this way doesn't make it the best way. We must be able to make those decisions for ourselves and adapt to the constant flow of change around us. Being stuck in a state of judgment prevents people from having a higher consciousness and adapting with grace to a constantly changing environment.

Accepting Others is Seeing Their Opinions

Connecting to those around you is bound to bring up some major differences. People have many opinions and often people disagree. So rather than try to convert your neighbor to your opinion or judge them, simply acknowledge that you never looked at it that way and you can see why they feel the way they do. You don't have to say that you agree, but simply that you see the person as they are. You give them space to be who they are. Being seen and accepted is a strong human need.

They may or may not ask your opinion, but I can guarantee that once you have their respect and trust, they will be more likely to listen to your opinion. You release judgment and simply accept them for who they are. You may not want to spend your free time with a person whose values are distinctly different from yours, but you also have a clear perception of who is around you. I'd rather know that a person has a belief structure different from mine than be around people pretending to be something they are not.

We are not meant to be clones. To me it's a celebration of our unique human condition, with each person contributing their own beautiful soul to the human collection. Celebrating differences empowers us to show our unique selves.

Freedom from Judgment Devotion

Dear Divine Source, Divinity, God, Goddess, Jesus, Soul Guides, or Loving Angels,

Please help me recognize my attempts to polarize and be aware of others trying to influence my opinions or control me. I thank my mind for trying to simplify my world by creating generalizations. I know that people who may challenge me can actually teach me or strengthen my discernment. Their opinions are not personal attacks on me. I will allow others to have opinions even if I can't understand why they feel the way they do. I trust my being to make choices based on love and for the betterment of this earth.

Thank you. Thank you. Thank you.

Holding Space Gives Grace

Making space for acceptance creates alignment with a higher mindset and moves us away from duality. Accepting each event for what it brings, without labeling it as "good" or "bad," would free us up to really feel what is going on and react from our hearts. It is either a desirable or undesirable situation or thing. Just because you don't like it doesn't make it bad or wrong. It's just not your thing.

Emotional Grace Devotion

Dear Divine Source, Divinity, God, Goddess, Jesus, Soul Guides, or Loving Angels,

I am perfect in design; every thought and feeling has a purpose. I am open to my connections in my body and choose to have awareness within myself. I choose balance to manage my emotions so I can act from a clear mind and make decisions based on grace and caring. My power from within originates from the highest good to help advance mankind to new awareness. Help me release judgments about my emotions and desires, letting them be fully felt and released for the greatest good. I act and speak from wisdom or wait until I feel balanced and aware. As I release self-judgments, I am more likely to be less judgmental of others.

I am Light. Light I am.

Thank you.

Two Sides to Every Story: Compassion for the Fallen

Free will has consequences. It can be hard to relate to choices we see others make. Here's a very sticky suggestion, but one that is very powerful in opening you up to living a life of love. Send light, love, and acceptance to the people whose actions make you upset. For example, you see a news article about a person who commits an armed robbery. You could get mad and consider how long they will be in jail. This lowers your energy frequency from love to judgment. I am not suggesting what the person did was good, but who are we to judge? Does your emotional reaction to anything or anyone else change anything? You may choose to have compassion for a person who was desperate. You may consider that the person could be mentally ill. As a society we have many broken people; they will have consequences for their actions. You can send them love to help them discern positive choices and support in breaking a cycle of violence.

Request to Support the Lost or Violent

Dear Angels,

Please send support and love to people in this world who are lost and violent. Wrap your loving wings around them so they can heal. Help those who are hurt by others; heal and forgive by shining your golden light of abundance around them. Help our society fix the broken systems that make people feel helpless and manipulated. Expose those who take advantage of the less fortunate and vulnerable.

We are one.

Thank you. Thank you. Thank you.

Chapter 12

Challenges Lead to Growth and Freedom in Forgiveness

With all the bravery needed to live in your heart center and without ego, you still will feel the sting of challenges in relationships. There are many times you will have to dust off your swollen, tender heart and make the choice to allow healing and forgiveness. Yes, a life of love is not all holding doors and rose petals. Sometimes you will feel like the door is slamming you in the face and all you receive from the roses are pricks from the thorns. People have free will and even with all your loving intentions, they may still choose actions that cause you pain, and almost even worse, be so clueless that they hurt you unintentionally. Sometimes people are just oblivious and thick-minded. Either way it's tough.

Why are You Upset?

Consider the idea that a fight is evidence that you and the other person have energy together. There is tension in your annoyance, and you care enough about that person to be really upset with them. The alternative is complete disregard and avoidance. I figure if I am getting in a fight with my partner, we still have some energy between us. The danger is when the conflict is not resolved or your stubbornness to be right, blinds you from your feelings of love. This tension needs an outlet, and you can harness it to bring you closer together or let it build up and drive you apart. Give yourself space to consider how you may be contributing to a conflict. Own your part. Trust that the conflict is there to teach you something about yourself and your partner. Try to express your feelings and hear them out. Try to realize their side of the hurt.

Feeling Triggered Devotion

Dear Divine Source, Divinity, God, Goddess, Jesus, Soul Guides, or Loving Angels,

Help me see how strong emotions take me out of my present moment and can make me react in defensive or hurtful ways. Help me feel this and give myself time and space to be calm and present. Help me use statements such as, "That is not what I am interested in right now," or "This situation is not working for me." Instead of being offended or hurt by something someone says to me, I can say, "Can you tell me more about what you just said? What did you mean?" If someone is judging me or trying to belittle me, help me see it as a sign of their insecurities. Putting their statement back on them, will either frustrate them or it may even reveal to them that they are coming across as negative toward me. People may disappoint me. Please help me realize that many times they are not aware. Send them light and love for the highest good.

I am clarity. Clarity I am.

Thank you. Thank you. Thank you.

You Have to Speak Your Reality

It's bound to happen. You feel strongly about someone. You have standards and opinions. Every relationship has tipping points. Communication is key. You must stand up and state that you are let down and angry. Pushing your hurt or frustration aside is going to do nothing for you. You can't afford to bury your unique feelings.

Help bring awareness to your relationship by using a phrase like: "Are you kidding me?" or "I would appreciate it if this never happened again, it really hurts me" or "I know you are not a mean person, but every time this happens, I feel like you are not considering me." "Maybe you hadn't thought about it, but your coming home late really makes it hard for me to get a good night's sleep. Do you think we could figure out a better time for you to come home?" Notice you are not name calling or accusing. You are simply stating your reality. Some people want you to simply tell them what to do and some people want to come up with solutions on their own. Maybe you need to come together to work out a solution together. You can ask them which they prefer.

Your partner should support your happiness. If they are only considering themselves, you have to figure out how that dynamic was established. Have you consistently put the needs of others first? Explore the dynamic and talk to your partner about how you feel. Being vulnerable about your needs and feelings will give them permission and space to be honest with you about their needs. Honoring your unique needs will bring you huge benefits. You have the opportunity to tell them how to show up for you. This may get messy, but you can't reach new levels in a relationship without diving into areas of weakness, attending to them, and moving on to a deeper connection.

Curiosity Brings a Vibration of Discovery and Problem Solving

Here's why it's important to know how to connect to your joy. Connecting with joy and finding humor in situations can help you defuse stress and confront your challenges with openness. You are here on earth to learn and evolve. There is no growth without obstacles and resistance. Facing these head on and owning the challenge takes bravery and guts. But please know, until you confront the challenge, own it, and make your decision to work through it, it will keep popping up.

Do you have recurring struggles in your relationships? You have the power to choose your approach. What if you stopped taking things personally and started asking questions? What if you became curious about your feelings and others' actions? At the same time, commit to being patient and compassionate to yourself. You see, it's a basic human need to be heard, acknowledged, and validated. Even if your questions are way off, you get a chance to see where the other person is coming from. Make space for them to meet you in a place of common caring. Come from a place of true curiosity and openness to their answer. If you ask the question from a state of accusation it will be taken as an attack. If attacking is your goal, you are basically telling the person you aren't ready to hear them, and your ego is so big you can't imagine how you might have also contributed to the situation. Can you recognize that your reactions can put you in a state of victimhood, which places all the blame on the other person? That's a whole lot of responsibility on the other person's shoulders! Feel free to read this paragraph again. I know I need to remind myself of this one quite often!

It's All About Perspective

So, my husband has a habit of shaking his wrist to readjust his watch. This seems like a very innocent thing and not something to get annoyed with. Right? Well, he does it when I am sitting close to him and oftentimes right in my face. I try to ignore it because he never bumps into me, and I know he would never hurt me. He is just adjusting his watch. I could tell it didn't even occur to him that it was annoying. I don't really remember how I brought it up, but I know that initially, I was so irritated that I couldn't find the words. I mean it's a whole arm movement; it's really intrusive and he was doing it on a regular basis. He really didn't even sense or realize that he was shaking his arm right in front of me. How rude! How can he be so unaware to shake his wrist right in my face without any regard to me?

I remember asking him if his watch needed to be sized. I remember moving away from him, which truly puzzled him. I remember staring at him when he did it. I remember making a noise every time he did it. I remember asking if I could sit on the other side of him. Finally, I unleashed my utter amazement at his lack of awareness and selfishness. I mean here I was sitting next to him trying to relax and he's shaking the whole couch with this arm. My goodness, he wasn't even checking the time! I am laughing about this now because he really was totally unaware, but I had to share my reality with him.

By holding it in, I was creating this wrist shaking monster! It was totally innocent, but also totally annoying. It's this way with many things in our relationship. He often is unaware and once I share my perspective in a calm, and neutral way: "Honey, do you realize, you are shaking your arm in my face?" he happily stops it. Now I get to make fun of it and laugh when he does it. Funny thing is that our son also has a habit of shaking his wrist to adjust his watch! When it first happened, we looked at each other in disbelief. It's a family joke now.

These are the gooey obstacles in which we lovingly make fun of each other. Moments that were once raw become silly memories that bond our love. I'm going to be real with you. It took time. I gave up being the victim, I let it go. I decided to laugh with him and stopped taking his actions as symbolic of whatever meaning my old fears wanted to perceive. It was my choice. It still took time. You have your own triggers. You have your own choices. What are you taking personally in your life that gives your power away? They may not go away, but with some awareness you can prevent them from stealing your joy.

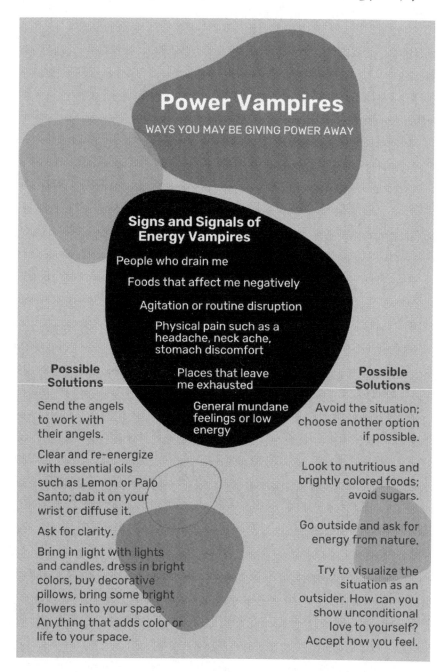

Power Vampires
WAYS YOU MAY BE GIVING POWER AWAY

Signs and Signals of Energy Vampires

People who drain me

Foods that affect me negatively

Agitation or routine disruption

Physical pain such as a headache, neck ache, stomach discomfort

Places that leave me exhausted

General mundane feelings or low energy

Possible Solutions

Send the angels to work with their angels.

Clear and re-energize with essential oils such as Lemon or Palo Santo; dab it on your wrist or diffuse it.

Ask for clarity.

Bring in light with lights and candles, dress in bright colors, buy decorative pillows, bring some bright flowers into your space. Anything that adds color or life to your space.

Possible Solutions

Avoid the situation; choose another option if possible.

Look to nutritious and brightly colored foods; avoid sugars.

Go outside and ask for energy from nature.

Try to visualize the situation as an outsider. How can you show unconditional love to yourself? Accept how you feel.

Spend some time with your list. Ask yourself how the frustration shows up in your body. Maybe it's a headache or a stiff neck. Whatever it is, you will know if you check in on your body. How can you look at this situation in a different light? Have you identified what bothers you about the situation? Be honest with yourself and decide if you want to share how you feel about the situation with the person or people involved. You can use a phrase like, "I'm not sure if you have noticed, but when you say you love me when you are walking out the door, it seems less genuine than when you look at me and say it. I'd really appreciate it if you stopped doing that because it really does hurt my feelings." Or "It may seem like a little thing to you, but it would help me out if you put the toilet paper on the hanger with the end facing out. I just don't like having to reach behind the roll to find the end." Sometimes it's bigger things like: "Can you help me out? I'm having trouble relating to your dad, can you tell me about why he may be doing this thing he does?" Or "Honey, the next time we make love, it would be totally the biggest turn on if you could say my name and look at me." Or "Can I share something with you? I know that many people are okay with porn but to me it really objectifies people, and it hurts me to see people's privacy invaded or broadcasted for entertainment."

Now these kinds of requests are sure to lead to bigger conversations, but the object is to get your partner talking and share your needs in a calm way. You have to start somewhere. Please don't judge your feelings as being selfish or ridiculous. Pushing your feelings aside will only give them time to move and grow from feelings to an explosive fight. Believe me it's better to deal with a few feelings than let them fester into or disruptions. You may discover new ways to bond and experience each other if you explore motivations for behaviors you don't identify with. By exposing difficult situations, we may just change the world. Once you can run through these feelings you create more space for joy. Ultimately your perception will decide if things continue to frustrate you, but sharing your reality helps others get to know your preferences and give them space to respond and support you in the relationship.

Sometimes the best strategy is to let some time pass. Get away from the situation so you have time to release your frustration, reflect, and recover.

Do you have the patience to wait

Till your mud settles and the water is clear?

Can you remain unmoving

Till the right action arises by itself?

~Lao Tzu

If you are a person of action and the thought of letting things settle makes you want to pull out your hair, I feel you. I can't do nothing when something is bothering me. So do something. If you are like me, a doer, my suggestion to you is to workout. You will be surprised how your frustration, anger, and hurt can translate into a great sweat. At first you may feel sluggish but stick with it. After your body adapts to what you are asking it to do and your mind starts to give in, you will feel a shift and you will feel power in the movement and release of the stress. You may even yell as you push yourself. Smile and feel how your body wants to show up for you. The conflict and hurt are real, but they don't need to stay with you. Be free.

My Needs Crossword

As you complete this puzzle, think about your needs and what you would add or take away. Words may be backwards, diagonal, up, or down. Enjoy!

My Needs

```
T  C  E  P  S  E  R  I  T  L
A  T  T  E  N  T  I  O  N  G
W  L  D  K  T  F  E  V  N  G
F  G  A  E  F  U  H  I  T  K
K  E  X  U  H  N  S  E  I  F
S  T  M  C  G  A  O  S  L  X
S  G  U  I  E  H  S  Z  I  P
X  O  U  T  T  E  T  T  K  T
T  Q  W  H  S  T  Q  E  I  M
P  R  E  S  E  N  T  S  R  Q
```

attention	teasing
hugs	kisses
presents	respect
text	time
fun	help
touch	laughter

Give Me Perspective Devotion

Dear Divine Source, Divinity, God, Goddess, Jesus, Soul Guides, or Loving Angels,

Help me to determine how conflict is affecting me. When I feel angry or hurt, where do these feelings come from? Please give me clarity in patterns so I can learn and release habits or interactions which no longer serve me. I want happiness and I realize my perception of people and knowledge of my own issues can help me through conflicts and lead to solutions. I am open to having a trusting and thoughtful relationship because I deserve it.

Thank you. Thank you. Thank you.

Have Good Intentions and Patience

Conflicts with friends or family can be stickier. I mean, when you are in a relationship, it's hard to be in constant conflict, so many times a relationship will heal, or it will run its course. However, friends and family stuff can simply fester or be easy to push aside because they may not be involved in your everyday life. It doesn't make it hurt less when they misunderstand you or make you feel insignificant. Being ignored or treated poorly by people who you think should love and understand you the most can be very upsetting. I am here to say, sometimes the Universe knows what is best for us and it throws us these situations not to test our strength, but to make space for new friendships and situations we would miss out on if we were in the old situation. I am not advocating to just pick up and leave your friends and family. However, if you have tried to make up, make amends, and express how you feel and they are letting you down or trying to control

135

you by leaving you without a resolution, it can be a dynamic that is keeping you from being your best self. I have often asked the angels to bring people into my life who will bring me to the highest expression of myself. I have become discerning about who I spend my time with. There is no need to tolerate people who don't get you just because you have a history with them. It's not fair to let them bring you down. It brings down the world.

It doesn't have to be a big thing of, "you did this to me," or "you made me feel like this." Just spend your time differently. Invest your energy in people and things that support you back. Be patient. You are not abandoning them. You are giving them time to grow at their own pace. It's not selfish, it's going with the flow. They may come around to you eventually. Cherish the times you had with them; pray for them to come meet you when they are ready, but don't lament something that doesn't work anymore. They were lucky to have your attention for that long!

Notice if there is a trend in things you would like to change. Many times, you will be challenged by things you need to master or look at differently. For example, if you have the same conflict with multiple friends, you may explore your belief system around that issue. Having the same issue with multiple people is a huge sign! Start to pay attention and you may be surprised. Or simply observe yourself and monitor your feelings throughout the day. If you get upset by a rude person who cuts you off in traffic, maybe you need to learn to not let your emotions be controlled by mindless people who do not know how to use their mirrors? What can your reactions tell you? Some people are just less aware, and I believe they have increased obstacles because of it. Can you be aware so you can diffuse, ignore, or avoid unwanted situations? Can you forgive yourself for being affected?

Wounds of the Past Devotion

Dear Divine Source, Divinity, God, Goddess, Jesus, Soul Guides, or Loving Angels,

I have old wounds. I have new wounds. I have wounds from other lifetimes. Give me space to look at those wounds and give thanks to those experiences. They taught me about relationships and myself. Now they are in the past. Even the wounds from five minutes ago are still in the past. I get this moment and every moment to make it what I want it to be. Help me see that living and protecting myself from old wounds, doesn't make them go away. I ask to be empowered by my past experiences and to live each day as it is with a renewed trust, a new chance at happiness and joyful living.

And so, it is.

Healing Takes Time

How do you move on from past hurt? It is not as easy as saying a devotion and simply moving on. You can spend your lifetime healing from a hurt. That's okay. The biggest thing is to recognize when wounds surface. Feel them rising to the surface. Honor them. You may even say something like, "I remember when _____. It happened. I lived through it and now it's over. I get a new chance." That thought, feeling, or memory came up at this moment. You don't have to go back to feeling the same way because you are not the same person you were then. You are the today you. Each moment you can define who you are. You get to choose your action or inaction at that moment. That's the magic of living. You get to decide your actions and your thoughts each time. You have free will. They are your responses and your emotions. Each emotion and each choice are individual and divine to you. Never let others' expectations define you. Tell yourself, "I am making space for this feeling, I honor it, but now I choose to let it go." Know that living in love gives you the power to change. You are not expecting others to change. It comes from you. Your behavior affects those around you. Your choices raise the level of consciousness in the people around you. Focus on love.

Message from the Angels for Self-Awareness

Dear One,

You have been given this day to use according to free will. Knowing your time is measured helps drive you to accomplish and gives inspiration. You have a unique contribution and ways only you can lift the love vibration. When you are uncomfortable having gratitude for yourself, start with those around you. See each person in your life as a gift. There are no accidents. Everyone you meet, befriend, hate, or avoid is there for you and you for them. The people who drive you crazy and irritate you are there to show you something about yourself. Pay attention. Take each encounter as an opportunity to connect with yourself in a new way. Showing that you are present to each person, even if you happen to make them irritated, gives you a reflection of yourself. If you can make a person smile, you smile. If the person is not open to your attention, all is well. See it and move on. Showing gratitude always comes back to self-love; everyone has their path.

You've got this!

Growth in the Struggle

Dr. Wayne Dyer, one of my favorites, has a book entitled Erroneous Zones. He teaches about things we do that are counterproductive to happiness. To me these habits fit into the old paradigm. In it, he talks about being externally centered or internally centered. People who tend to blame others for their feelings or situations are the most unhappy. People who feel control and recognize that they are allowing themselves to be triggered or recognize what they have contributed to the situation and learn from it, tend to be more in control of their emotions and happier. To me it's about loving and trusting yourself to really tune into what is happening. Things that trigger you are the things that will keep triggering you until you figure it out. It's about facing fear and surrendering to it. When you own the messy parts of yourself and hold yourself accountable, you can get to a place of great love and complete grace. You become the master of yourself because you took the time to tune in, be present, and care with an attitude of achievement. You are not broken because you struggle. You struggle because you long to reach your divinity and be whole.

Rising Up From Falling Down Devotion

Dear Divine Source, Divinity, God, Goddess, Jesus, Soul Guides, or Loving Angels,

Give me the feeling of joy from my favorite memory and help me feel the freedom of bliss. I may let my spirit sink into despair and it's okay. I can use my memory to anchor into a higher feeling or use the hurt to drive me to take action. All emotions are essential, and I respect what each feeling is there to teach me. I especially cherish the pain and suffering because it shows me how I can, through free will, have compassion for others and connect to them with love and understanding. I know that when I fall down, I can get up and go higher than before.

And so, it is.

Transform Pain to Power

Hurt is real and you must feel it. Feeling it and letting it go is essential. Holding on to or pretending the hurt doesn't exist results in blocks of your energy that prevent you from forgiving and healing. When you feel pain, you may be tempted to tell yourself you are being sensitive, or you should get over it. You may even try to convince yourself it isn't a big deal. In contrast, beating yourself up about feeling hurt will never resolve it. It takes bravery and strength to have courage to accept your feelings as they are. Once you accept them you can be creative as to how to heal the hurt and grow stronger.

You may have had hard times. You may have sensed that what you were getting into was trouble, but you did it anyway. That is awesome. Instead of feeling like you made a mistake and beating yourself up for knowing better but not doing better, compliment yourself on having a feeling about it and resolve to listen to your gut instinct next time and trust it. Guidance and intuition surround you. Sometimes we just need another try.

Getting Beyond and Rising Up Devotion

Dear Divine Source, Divinity, God, Goddess, Jesus, Soul Guides, or Loving Angels,

I am here at the place where I sit knowing that I have more. My spirit is tested. My will can be so weak. I take a deep breath and feel that I am not alone. My soul tugs my shirt. My will is not broken. All I can see is the darkness, yet I search for light. My eyes burn searching for some rest. I am here at the bottom of the pit again. I breathe so I cannot accept the darkness. I will not be complacent. I yearn for the sun, the warmth. My eyes lift. My heart can mend. I call in love, it starts as a whisper, a faint caress, a slight whip of a breeze in my face. I breathe in deeply and call-in love once again. This time my heart swells with warmth and I push out the pain. I breathe in light and push out the darkness. The memory of the hurt builds my resolve. I am weak at times, but then I remember. I remember my heart, my mission. My divine purpose propels me to rise. I dust off my legs, straighten my top, and draw my shoulders back and down. I am strong. I call in love and open my heart. Nothing can close down my heart. My cells sing and vibrate with illumination. I am not alone.

And so, it is.

Thank you. Thank you. Thank you.

Freedom in Self-Forgiveness

Although we are called by our soul to love and be loved and we know our bodies are sacred gifts to cherish, we can forget. Many times, we choose love, joy, and health. However, there are times, through free will, we take a path that leads to pain and suffering. It was a choice we made. Living through suffering leads to compassion and awareness. When you are open to the lesson and accept that it was you who chose it, you are not a victim. You went to the pain and suffering, you chose that path, and it was perfect because now you know. It was a choice!

Regret Clouds the Lesson

There have been times you have made choices you would never make again. Times you have given away your power, your identity, and your will to people who did not appreciate or cherish you in ways you know you deserve. I call on you to recognize that even though you regret the choices you made, those instances were there to show you what you were not okay with. They made you stronger to identify what you want and don't want. If you repeat the mistake, you will continue to make that mistake until you level with yourself and build your resolve to make the choice that makes your heart sing and not shrink.

Forgiveness Devotion

Dear Divine Source, Divinity, God, Goddess, Jesus, Soul Guides, or Loving Angels,

Please guide me to forgive. I know that my body can hold onto hurt and replay situations over and over in effort to protect me. Please help me locate where I may be holding onto hurt. I surrender to that hurt and ask to release it. I forgive the person and situation which was hurtful to me. I release any contribution I may have made consciously or unconsciously.

Thank you. Thank you. Thank you.

People Can Be Clueless. Kindly Share Your Reality.

Forgiveness makes room for solutions for yourself and everyone else around you. Even though people can seem rude and selfish, rarely is any person trying to hurt your feelings. Mostly people are just trying to get through their day and take care of their own needs. They don't have the mindset to think about how their actions may affect you or what they may look like. Most people are self-absorbed and only considerate when they are in the spotlight, such as in social situations where they feel pressure to perform, dating, job interviews, and work relationships in which they are trying to get ahead. With that said, rarely are people trying to hurt you, unless they are just mean (and frankly you would have picked up on the fact that the person you are with is mean). If they aren't mean and just acting like an ass, it's up to you to blow it off and forgive them or decide that this behavior is unacceptable, and you can't stand it. Please know that they may be shocked that you feel the way you do and deny what happened. It's true; it's all about perception. Thoughts create your reality. If you see that person as someone who is just trying to get through their day with little awareness for what is going on, it's much easier to say something non-threatening like, "Hey, I am right here and I would like some attention," accompanied by a caress of their back. That kind of approach will bring you more of what you want than slamming a dish in the dishwashing or being short with them. Your positive energy will draw them to you.

An ancient Hawaiian ceremony called *Ho'oponopono* is traditionally practiced by a group of people involved in a crisis. The practice centers on forgiveness, redemption, and healing followed by a symbolic meal. The mantra which is repeated can be used by individuals to forgive themselves and others and has been shown to be transformational by many. These words are repeated until the parties involved feel better and there is nothing left to heal:

I love you.

I'm sorry.

Please forgive me.

Thank you.

In repeating these powerful statements in a mantra, feelings and events will start to surface. One at a time you can work through them and release them. Sending them on their way so they no longer weigh you down and you are free to heal and love.

Openness to Take a Fresh Perspective

What if you entered every situation with an open heart and observation, even the situations in which you feel you have experienced a thousand times? Those Groundhog Day moments of mundane in which you just know what is going to happen can be telling. There is no change until there is an underlying difference. In order to make a situation change, something has to shake it up. It can be something very subtle. A pause, a smile, or perhaps a new inquiry can change the whole dynamic. This also creates space for you to be in the situation in a different way. People don't change because you ask them to or because it's the right thing to do. People change because they look at something in a different way or see a potential they didn't know about before. When you are open to a new perspective, you invite curiosity and possibilities you couldn't have predicted. You can create real change just by being totally present in your life. Rushing around completing your to-do list only accomplishes a to-do list. Boring. A life of love takes place while you are completing your to-do list and in the small moments all around you. Joy.

Highest Expression of Myself Devotion

Dear Divine Source, Divinity, God, Goddess, Jesus, Soul Guides, or Loving Angels,

I am a divine being and I trust and respect myself; my choices and relationships reflect my great respect for myself and my relationships. I joyfully explore my heart and desires. Others wish to be there for me and show up in the highest vibration possible. I recognize others around me as divine beings.

And so, it is.

Thank you. Thank you. Thank you.

Chapter 13

Standards and Your Resolve

Standards and Discernment

Once you start to shine your divinity to the world, there will be people who are drawn to your light and energy. You will feel the attraction. At times, it may seem like an imposition. You need to be aware. Not everyone has a clear loving intention. I have had men follow me in parking lots and at the grocery store. At times I could tell they were harmless but at other times, I have needed to exit quickly. As you become more aware of your effect on the people around you, you will sense any threat or return their smile with a nice comment. Most people are kind and just want to be noticed in a playful way. It's a subtle thing.

Your ability to discern what is good for you will become fine-tuned. Your spirit of love and acceptance will bring people into your life who are looking for the same qualities. Your vibe will be noticeable. You now have a lens to view your world. Your values and instincts will reveal what is best for you. These standards give you a structure and when unwanted situations occur, you can choose to engage or simply exit and avoid. Things may simply feel off. It's up to you to be creative to find out how to return, rebalance, and align with your love. Less time will be spent in frustration because you are viewing your world with a focus on abundance and hope because your standards are aligned with a life of love.

Your standards are not just going to be centered around the people and situations, but also the things you allow into and around your body. You may be more sensitive to foods, activities, or violent entertainment. You can trust your body to guide you to what's best for you. Be gentle and compassionate to your needs. Your balanced, happy body serves as a sacred container. It's the foundation for how you are present for yourself.

Setting Standards Devotion

Dear Divine Source, Divinity, God, Goddess, Jesus, Soul Guides, or Loving Angels,

I recognize that I need clear standards; I may be able to express them clearly or I may need time to define them. Help me see situations in which I have lacked standards. Give me awareness to set clear limits on the ways I allow others to use my resources. I am in control of how I give my gifts. When I communicate my standards, they need to be respected. If others ignore or pressure me, I can easily move away from them, so they no longer have access to me. I find it easy to say, "This doesn't work for me anymore," or "No thank you." I only accept those who respect my standards and cherish my time. I am valuable and precious. I am love.

And so, it is.

Thank you. Thank you. Thank you.

Self-Care

Self-care requires standards and awareness. You may be prone to over-giving. Frankly it's often easier to focus on helping others than honestly looking at yourself. Anytime you feel taken for granted, frustrated, or overwhelmed, that's a sign you need some self-care. Simply, those feelings of lack are glowing, neon signs. Stop and care for your needs. You are the most important person. Your state of balance provides the highest expression for how you show up for others. You can be creative, loving, and joyful from your place of peace and balance. This way of living brings in abundance while radiating peace and love to those around you. Protect your innocence and divine, loving vibration like it's a cherished puppy or a delicate infant.

Standards are Unique to You

Part of realizing your power and the impact of love in your life is the application of a decision. Typically, we are pushed into a place of no return when we are forced to decide just because we simply cannot take it anymore. Your decision is your standard. What if you have old standards that no longer serve you? Maybe you keep finding yourself in the same situation. I would like to think of standards as something that your heart determines in the moment. They are not walls put up to protect you. However, they represent freedom to defend and protect your values and desires. Something snaps inside you that says enough is enough, and you decide to make it unacceptable. Standards can also be based on your values and purpose for living. If you don't stand for something, you will fall for anything. What are you willing to stand up for? As you connect with your higher self and more light and love, you will find some old habits no longer serve you. You will notice small things others will miss. You will feel deeply at times, and it will be uncomfortable at times. But you will also have much more joy and a lightening of your heart with little unexpected things. You will pick up on emotions and trends before others. This will take patience. It may be frustrating as what is obvious to you will be hidden from others. This is all good and a sign you are living a life of love.

Message from the Angels About Being Different

Dear One,

We have connected with you. You have connected to us. It is a blessing. We are blessed by you, and you are blessed by us. You will not want to go back to your old, unfeeling self. Although there will be times you will feel low and heavy, we will help you. We will guide you. Please ask us to raise you up; just fill your mind with a column of light and love. This life can be so dense, but we can offer illumination and clarity. It is all within you. We want to give you a lens for clarity. We know you feel it. You are different and different in your world can be hard. It can be challenging to be different, but your differences are what the world needs right now. You may not understand how your differences are helping heal and transform your world, but they are, and you are important. You, living in your strength, your expression, your creativity, and your divine feminine, can heal this world. You cannot heal this world by being part of a flock. No, my dear you must be your radiant, unique, strong, and powerful self. Yes, this is what will change the world. Be patient while the rest of the earth catches up. We will giggle with delight with you as your eyes sparkle with recognition.

And so, it is.

Resolve

Your commitment to a life of love can start today. Review your values from chapter two and pleasures from chapter four to create a mission statement for your life. Get out a pen and write it down on paper. Once you write it out, your reality can be rooted in your timeline. This is not a step-by-step linear process of an a + b = c. Think about your life as an upward spiral of progression. As you practice living in your joy and being focused on love, you will experience bolts of progress. How do you know you are making progress? You will feel lighter. You will feel healthier. You will notice things happening for you. People will show up for you in ways you never dreamed.

Once you decide why you want to love and how you want to support yourself for the highest good, you will find strength and resolve to stand up for what you believe in. You will have courage to speak from a loving heart because you know grace and you extend that grace not only to yourself but everything around you. You will no longer consider, "What will they think of me if I say this?" You will say it from a balanced and centered heart without fear. This demonstrates clarity around what is right for you.

A life of love is supported through perseverance, a dedication to live life at a high vibration. This high vibration is achieved by honoring yourself, calling in love, and envisioning the highest possible outcome for yourself and those around you. This looks different to each person. However, a life of love is self-sustaining. Once you feel the joy of loving this way, you will want more of it. In times you fall from your sensual, compassionate heart and into pain or hurt, you will feel a pull to return to a life of love. Love isn't dependent on situations or people outside of you, but a reality you create through your loving connections. Your love is constantly growing and evolving.

How Sensuality Fits In

Sensuality is something everyone is born with, but we may have forgotten. The best way to remember and build on your sensuality is through self-love. Through self-care of eating the best foods, getting the right kind of rest, exercising, and honoring your beautiful body, you can be open to your most sensual feelings. The knowledge that you alone can love the way you do is empowering. Your sensuality connects you to the divine feminine and is a source of abundance and deep joy. Think of it as the best hug that you ever gave, except you are giving it to yourself. If you choose to share your sensuality physically, that person is very lucky indeed. Your sensuality is a gift filled with expression and joy and it's the ultimate way you creatively express your love to the world.

Your connection to your body and the earth below you support a life of love. When you take care of the earth you are taking care of your tenderness, your sensuality, and your connectedness to it all. Arousal is a symptom of your ability to feel and be felt in the world around you. When you ignore parts of this world, you are ignoring parts of yourself. Sensing what is happening around you opens your awareness and ability to feel. Sometimes it hurts and it's uncomfortable to really see what is going on around you. You may realize some things around you that you would like to change. Maybe you notice a neighbor who has a short temper with his children, an elderly woman who has a hard time walking, or a neighbor who needs to vent about a bad situation at work. People may be hesitant to be involved in their community for fear of being called nosey or a busy body but having local connections in your community and knowing about events in your area could make all the difference. We simply cannot keep living like each one of us is an island when there are ways can be there for each other.

You have divine knowledge or intuition on your side, knowing what is best for you at every moment. The more you can cherish and protect your sovereign knowledge and love yourself, the more you will attract the same kind of love from those around you. Remember love is your birthright; you never have to earn it. From this knowledge you follow your heart and your joy. Your joy is your unique gift to the world. It's a precious treasure. Do not worry if you have times of weakness or periods of pain. Your magical life can help you spend less time in the unwanted states. You will bounce back to your highest self more quickly. When you despair, try to remember your divinity and know you are a cherished soul. To remember your divinity, draw your attention to your values and pay attention to the spark in you that keeps your breath flowing. That's your purpose. Attention creates flow. Do not focus your attention on what is lacking, but on what you have and keep giving your attention to that. You desire more, so your attention will draw in the abundance which is your highest good. I love you. The angels and your spiritual team are here with you. Keep calling them close. No request is too small. Your efforts to have a better life will change the world.

Message from the Angels for Encouragement

Dear One,

You are a divine being. You show up, you are living and breathing and that is a sign you are part of a great design. You may not know what your path will bring, but if you can trust and keep stepping forward, it will be revealed to you. You are making a difference just by reading this book. Your love energy will increase, and it will spread to those you are in contact with if they are ready for it. You are feeling better every day and taking steps to make your life more joyful, more loving. That is positive change, and you are part of the Loving Revolution. We, the Council of Light and the Archangels thank you and are here supporting you. When you are feeling down, please ask us to support you. Place your hand out and we will fill it with courage and love.

And so, it is.

Love Conquers All

Your life of love inspires others to love. It's the ultimate service to our world and everything depends on it. We cannot survive on this planet without showing and sharing love. The environment depends on us loving each other enough to care about what our neighbors, our country, and people in other countries are going through. When we teach our children to care about their needs, respect themselves, each other, and the planet, we are ensuring survival and strong communities. Our survival is dependent on our ability to help each other, while maintaining a strong self-identity and liberty. There's a constant tension. We have corporate machines designed to employ us and make money, but in our communities it's up to us to reclaim humanity and balance out the power of profit over humanity. We must preserve liberty in our communities because there is no joy in surrendering your power to an institution. Just listen to the birds singing. They want us to hear the message. They sing for us, encouraging us to make a shift. Just listen to the water flowing. It wants to cleanse us and make things right.

You are a powerful being of light and transformation. You are always learning, adapting, and growing. You have connected to amazing resources. There are no limits to your loving soul and no quota for your joy in this life. This connection is available to you at all times. All you have to do is ask, receive, and act. Being abundant, happy, and free are your birthrights!

Every new moment is a chance to create a life of love. Be gentle with yourself. Give grace and honor feelings of peace. When you take quiet moments to find peace in your heart those moments turn into much bigger things in your life. There is no limit to your abundance once you determine what your joy and heart really desire. This new earth depends on our divine, loving hearts to guide it to be a place of acceptance and honor where every person is free to follow their joy. Every voice is cherished and heard. For when our voices come together, we create a symphony of souls. My soul dances with delight when I envision the adventures ahead of you in your Life of Love.

Thank You

This book may just be the beginning of your transformational journey. I invite you to subscribe to my Podcast: Life of Love a Joyful Guide to Self and Sensuality. Also, if my messages resonate with you and you wish to have individual support or more in-depth guidance, I am here for you as a Life of Love coach. For more information and to receive the latest updates, visit my website: www.youneedapeptalk.com.

Thank you. Thank you. Thank you.

Index of Angel Messages

Index of Actions and Exercises

Index of Devotions

Acknowledgments

Many thanks to my parents who nurtured, loved, and protected me. They were my first and most impressionable love, giving me a stable, loving foundation, and many freedoms to explore my heart and mind. Their loving relationship, while raising four quite different but all extremely active children, is something I adore and often admire. I cherish my loving family and everything they have taught me.

To my husband, Mitch, who has loved and supported me through many ups and downs: you are my best friend, my love, my rock, and my biggest rival at times. Loving you has taught me so much about myself. Thanks for challenging me and encouraging me to jump in and share this book.

To my sons, Reese and Blake: loving you fulfills me. I have always wanted to be your mother. I am in awe of the ways you bring such depth to my love. Please know that my biggest joy is seeing you share love in the world with strength and honesty. I am a warrior for your future, as I wish to see a world in which every person is free to share love in a way that builds a world full of compassion, respect, and honor.

This book would not have been possible without the generous support of Dr. Carolyn Porter. She is my spiritual mentor who opened the gates of angel blessings and awareness to me. I hold dear our monthly angel meetings and the members of the Angel Hood.

The angels have been with me through everything. I created this book through their guidance and perseverance. They gave me signs of validation when I had doubts as well as inspiration when I waivered. I am so grateful for their loving presence in my life. I know that Archangel Michael is fighting for and supporting humankind in our rise of consciousness. He was very influential in the writing of this book.

It has become very hard to ignore the synchronicities in my life. The support and connections that were revealed to me during the process of writing this book have been simply magical. I will be forever grateful to the Birth Your Legacy Conscious Leaders Conference produced by Danielle Rama Hoffman that I attended in the Spring of 2020. My life path was illuminated when I heard her channel Thoth and the Council of Light. The Birth Your Legacy Conference also connected me to Michelle Vandepas and her team at GracePoint Publishing. Her message about living my divine purpose inspired me to share my love language through this book. Michelle then introduced me to Shauna Hardy, my creative editor. She read my words, saw my vision, and inspired me to really share from my heart. I know the angels matched us up as we easily understand each other. I hope you feel the love and care I took in writing this book. I can't wait to hear about how the angels work in your life and how this book lives in you.

About the Author

Julie Hilsen has spent her life in the love vibration. From an early age, she was empathically connected with people of all ages, origins and creeds. Her Master's in Communication Sciences and connections to Spirit are blended within her book to share secrets about creating a unique life of deep, expansive love. She is a certified Angel Practitioner, intuitive and transformational coach.

Julie lives in Cumming, Georgia with her husband of 20 years, their sons Reese and Blake as well as their fur baby, Sydney. She enjoys cooking, playing tennis, golfing, gardening, and taking long hikes in the forest. When the weather doesn't cooperate to be outside, she enjoys the inspiration and sweat that the Peloton bike brings. Her leaderboard handle is Georgia_Dreamer. She also enjoys coaching and coordinating as a volunteer for Special Pops, a nonprofit for promoting adaptive tennis for Special Olympic athletes. Her intention for living a healthy, creative, joyful, and sensual life has been illuminated by the Counsel of Light and many Angelic entities. She shares their messages and guidance with you as it is her pleasure to teach others to connect to their divine wisdom and angelic guides. As when one of us is happy, we shine that happiness out into our world, and we are transformed.

"This day is a gift and each moment a new beginning." — *Julie Hilsen*

For more great books, please visit GracePoint Publishing online at
books.gracepointpublishing.com.

If you enjoyed reading *Life of Love: A Joyful Guide to Self and Sensuality*
and purchased it through an online retailer, please return to the site
and leave a review or rating to help others find this book.

Made in the USA
Columbia, SC
27 November 2022